Society Against The State

Translated by Robert Hurley

in collaboration with Abe Stein

Society Against The State

Essays in Political Anthropology

Pierre Clastres

ZONE BOOKS · NEW YORK

1987

ZONE BOOKS
New York, New York

Originally published as
La Société contre l'état

Printed in Canada

Distributed by The MIT Press,
Cambridge, Massachusetts, and London, England

Library of Congress Catalog Card Number: 87-50396

ISBN 0-942299-00-0

Contents

Copernicus and the Savages

Someone said to Socrates that a
certain man had grown no better in
his travels. "I should think
not," he said. "He took himself
along with him."

Montaigne

Can serious questions regarding power be asked? A fragment of *Beyond Good and Evil* begins: "Inasmuch as in all ages, as long as mankind has existed, there have also been human herds (clans, communities, tribes, peoples, states, churches), and always a great number who obey in comparison with the small number who command – in view, therefore, of the fact that obedience has been most practiced and fostered among mankind hitherto, one may reasonably suppose that the need for it is now innate in everyone, as a kind of *formal conscience* which gives the command: 'Thou shalt unconditionally do something, unconditionally refrain from something'; in short, 'Thou Shalt.'" Unconcerned as he often is about the true and false in his sarcasm, Nietzsche in his way, nonetheless, isolates and accurately defines a field of reflection once consigned to speculative thought alone, but which for roughly two decades has been entrusted to truly scientific research.

At issue is the space of the *political*, at whose center *power* poses its questions: new themes – new in social anthropology – of a growing number of studies. That ethnology so belatedly developed an interest in the political dimension of archaic societies – its preferential object, after all – is, as I shall try to show, something not alien to the very problematic of power. It is, rather, evidence of a spontaneous mode, immanent to our culture and therefore very traditional, of understanding the political relations that proliferate in other societies. But the lag is being compensated for, the deficiencies made good. There are now enough texts and descriptions so that one may speak of a political anthropology, measure its findings, and reflect on the nature of power, its source, and the transformations history forces upon it, depending on the types of society in which it is exercised.

It is an ambitious project, but also a necessary task, one accomplished in J. W. Lapierre's substantial work, *Essai sur le fondement du pouvoir politique.*[1] It is an undertaking all the more worthy of interest since this book assembles and applies a body of information concerning not just human societies but the social animal species as well; moreover, its author is a philosopher whose mind is brought to bear on the data provided by the modern disciplines of "animal sociology" and ethnology.

It is then the question of political power and, quite justifiably, J. W. Lapierre asks first whether this human fact corresponds to any vital necessity; whether it unfolds from biological roots; whether – in other words – power has its birthplace and raison d'etre in nature and not in culture. At the end of a patient and

1. J. W. Lapierre, *Essai sur le fondement du pouvoir politique*, Publication de la Faculté d'Aix-en-Provence, 1968.

informed discussion of the latest work in animal biology – a discussion not at all academic, although predictable in its outcome – the answer is clear: "The critical examination of acquired knowledge regarding social phenomena among animals, and in particular regarding their processes of self-regulation, has shown us the absence of any form, even embryonic, of political power ..." (p. 212). By clearing this terrain, the author has secured his inquiry against the risk of exhausting itself in that direction. He can then turn to the sciences of culture and history in order to examine the "archaic" forms of political power in human societies. The thoughts that follow were especially prompted by a reading of those pages devoted to power among the Savages.

The range of societies considered is impressive, wide enough to dispel any doubts the exacting reader might have as to the exhaustive nature of the sampling, since the analysis is based on examples taken from Africa, the three Americas, the South Sea Islands, Siberia, and so on. In short, given its geographical and typological variety, an all but complete anthology of every difference the "primitive" world might offer in comparison with the non-archaic horizon; the latter serving as the background against which looms the shape of political power in our culture.

It might easily be thought that all these dozens of societies have in common is the archaism ascribed to them. But this is a negative definition, as Lapierre points out, established by the absence of writing and the so-called subsistence economy. Therefore, archaic societies can differ profoundly among themselves. Here we are far removed from the dreary repetition that would paint all Savages gray.

Thus, a minimum of order must be introduced into this multiplicity to allow for comparison among the units that compose it. This is why Lapierre, more or less accepting the classic classifications proposed by Anglo-Saxon anthropology, conceives five major types: "starting from archaic societies in which political power is most developed so as to arrive finally at those which exhibit . . . almost no political power, or none in the strict sense of the term" (p. 229). Primitive cultures, therefore, are arranged in a typology based on the greater or lesser "quantity" of political power each of them affords to observation, this quantity of power being capable of approaching zero: ". . . some human groups, given living conditions enabling them to subsist in small 'closed societies,' have managed to do without political power" (p. 525).

Let us reflect on the principle itself of this classification. What is its criterion? How does one define the thing, present in greater, or lesser quantity, that makes it possible to assign a given place to a given society? In other words, what is meant, if only provisionally, by political power? The question is undeniably important, since the interval presumed to separate societies without power from those with it ought simultaneously to disclose the essence of power and its basis. Now, in following Lapierre's analyses, their thoroughness notwithstanding, one does not have the impression of being witness to a break, a discontinuity, a radical leap that, wrenching the human groups from their pre-political stagnation, would transform them into a civil society. Does this mean that between societies with a + sign and those with a − sign the transition is gradual, continuous, and quantitative in nature? Were such the case, the very possibility of classifying societies would vanish, for between the two extremes – societies with a state and societies without power – there would appear an infinity of intermediate degrees, conceivably turning each particular society into a single class of the system. Moreover, a similar fate is in store for every taxonomic scheme of this kind as knowledge about archaic societies improves and their differences come increasingly to light. Consequently, whether we assume discontinuity between non-power and power, or continuity, it appears that no classification of empirical societies can enlighten us either on the nature of power or the circumstances of its advent, so that the riddle remains in all its mystery.

"Power is realized within a typical social relationship: command-obedience (p. 44)." From which it directly follows that societies where this essential relationship is not observed are societies without power. I will return to this idea. Worth noting first is the traditionalism of a concept that quite faithfully expresses the spirit of ethnological inquiry: namely, the unquestioned conviction that political power is manifested within a relation that ultimately comes down to coercion. On this score the kinship is closer than seems apparent between Nietzsche, Max Weber (state power as the monopoly of the legitimate use of violence), and contemporary ethnology. And the difference in their respective languages means less than their common point of departure: the truth and reality of power consists of violence; power cannot be conceptualized apart from its predicate: violence. Perhaps that is how things really are, in which case ethnology should not be blamed for uncritically accepting what the West has always believed. But the point is that it is necessary to ascertain and verify on the terrain involved – that of archaic societies – whether, when there is neither coercion nor violence, it is impossible to speak of power.

What are the facts about the Indians of America? It is known that, with the exception of the Highland cultures of Mexico, Central America, and the Andes, all the Indian societies are archaic: they are ignorant of writing and they live, economically speaking, on a subsistence level. Further, all, or almost all, are headed by leaders, chiefs, and – this decisive feature merits attention – none of these caciques possesses any "power." One is confronted, then, by a vast constellation of societies in which the holders of what elsewhere would be called power are actually without power; where the political is determined as a domain beyond coercion and violence, beyond hierarchical subordination; where, in a word, no relationship of command-obedience is in force. This is the major difference of the Indian world, making it possible to speak of the American tribes as a homogeneous universe despite the extreme diversity of the cultures moving within it. Thus, according to Lapierre's criterion, the New World in its virtual entirety would fall into the pre-political sector, that is, into the last group of his typology which contains those societies where "political power approaches zero."

Nothing of the sort is true, however, since the classification in question is punctuated with American examples. Indian societies are included in all the types, and few among them happen to belong to the last type which normally ought to contain them all. This involves some misunderstanding since one has a choice of two things: either chieftainships with power are found in some societies, i.e., chiefs who on giving an order see it executed, or it does not exist. Now direct field experience, the monographs of researchers, and the oldest chronicles leave no room for doubt on this score: if there is something completely alien to an Indian, it is the idea of giving an order or having to obey, except under very special circumstances such as prevail during a martial expedition. Why do the Iroquois appear in the first category, alongside the African kingships? Can the Great Council of the League of the Iroquois be likened to "a state that is still rudimentary but already constituted"? For if "the political concerns the functioning of the entire society" (p. 41), and if "exercising a power is *to decide for the whole group*" (p. 44), then it cannot be said that the 50 sachems who composed the Iroquois Great Council constituted a state. The League was not a total society but a political alliance of five total societies, the five Iroquois tribes. The British typologies of African societies are perhaps relevant to the black continent, but they cannot serve as a model for America because, let it be repeated, there is no essential difference between the Iroquois sachem and the leader of the smallest nomad band. And it should be pointed out that while the Iroquois confederation rightly arouses the interest of specialists, there were attempts elsewhere, less noteworthy because they were sporadic, at forming tribal leagues by the Tupi-Guarani of Brazil and Paraguay, among others.

The above remarks are intended to problematize the traditional form in which the problematic of power is posed. It is not evident to me that coercion and subordination constitute the essence of political power *at all times and in all places*. Consequently, an alternative presents itself: either the classic concept of power is adequate to the reality it contemplates, in which case it must account for non-power wherever it is located; or it is inadequate and must be discarded or transformed. However, it is pertinent at the outset to probe the mental attitude that allows such a concept to develop. And for this purpose the vocabulary of ethnology itself is capable of putting us on the right track.

First of all, let us examine the criteria that define archaism: the absence of writing and subsistence economy. Nothing need be said about the first, since it involves an admitted fact: either a society is familiar with writing or it is not. On the other hand, the relevance of the second criterion appears less certain. Actually, what does "subsistence" mean? It means living in a permanently fragile equilibrium between alimentary needs and the means for satisfying them. A society with a subsistence economy, then, is one that barely manages to feed its members and thus finds itself at the mercy of the slightest natural accident (drought, flood, etc.); a decline in its resources would automatically make it impossible to feed everyone. In other words, archaic societies do not live, they survive; their existence is an endless struggle against starvation, for they are *incapable of producing a surplus* because of technological and – beyond that – cultural deficiency. Nothing is more persistent than this view of primitive society, and at the same time nothing is more mistaken. If it has become possible recently to speak of groups of paleolithic hunters and gatherers as "the first affluent societies,"[2] how will "neolithic"[3] agriculturalists be described? This is not the place to dwell on a question of crucial importance for ethnology. Let it be remarked merely that a good many of those archaic societies "with a subsistence economy," in South America, for example, produced a quantity of *surplus* food often *equivalent* to the amount required for the annual consumption of the community: a production capable, therefore, of satisfying its needs twice over, or capable of feeding a population twice its size. Obviously that does not mean that archaic societies are not archaic; the aim is simply to puncture the "scientific" conceit of the concept of the subsistence economy, a concept that reflects the attitudes and habits of Western observers with regard to primitive societies more than the economic reality on which those cultures are based. In any case, it is not because they had a subsistence economy that archaic societies "have survived in a state of extreme underdevelopment up to the present time" (p. 225). In fact, it strikes me that, using this standard, the illiterate and undernourished European proletariat of the nineteenth century would be more aptly described as archaic. In reality, the notion of the subsistence economy belongs to the ideological purview of the modern West, and not at all to the conceptual store of a science. And it is paradoxical to see ethnology become the victim of such a crude mystification, something especially dangerous inasmuch as ethnology has had a part in orienting the strategy of the industrialized nations vis-à-vis the so-called underdeveloped world.

2. Marshall Sahlins, "La Première Société d'abondance," *Les Temps Modernes*, no. 268 (October 1968), pp. 641–80.

3. Regarding the problems raised by a definition of the neolithic, see last chapter.

The objection will be raised that everything which has been said really has little bearing on the problem of political power. On the contrary: the same outlook that gives rise to talk of primitive peoples as being "men living with difficulty in a subsistence economy, in a state of technical underdevelopment" (p. 319) also determines the meaning and the tone of the familiar discourse regarding power and political life. Familiar in that the encounter between the West and the Savages has always been an occasion for repeating the same discourse concerning them. Witness, for example, how the first European explorers of Brazil described the Tupinamba Indians: "People without god, law, and king." Their *mburuvicha*, or chiefs, actually had no "power." What could be stranger, for people coming out of societies in which authority culminated in the absolute monarchies of France, Portugal, or Spain? They were confronted by barbarians who did not live in civilized society. In contrast, their anxiety and irritation at finding themselves in the presence of the abnormal disappeared in Montezuma's Mexico or in the Peru of the Incas. There the conquistadors could breathe the same old air, a most stimulating atmosphere for them of hierarchies, coercion – in a word, of genuine power. Now a remarkable continuity can be observed between that ungracious, artless, and one might say savage discourse, and that of present-day scholars and researchers. The judgment is the same though couched in more delicate terms, and one finds under Lapierre's signature a number of expressions consistent with the most common perception of political power in primitive societies. Take the following example: "Do not the Trobriander or Ticopian 'chiefs' hold a social authority and an economic power that is very developed, as opposed to a truly political power that is quite *embryonic*? (p. 284)." Or: "No Nilotic people has been able to rise to the level of the centralized organizations of the great Bantu kingdoms (p. 365)." And also: "Lobi society *has been unable to* create a political organization

(p. 435, note 134)."[4] What is implied by this kind of vocabulary in which the words "embryonic," "nascent," "poorly developed" frequently appear? The object is not to force a quarrel with an author, for I am well aware that this is the very language of anthropology. What is wanted is access to what might be called the archeology of this language and the knowledge that professes to emerge by means of it. The question being raised is: what exactly is this language saying and what is the locus from which it says the things it is saying?

We have seen that the idea of a subsistence economy purports to be a factual appraisal, but it involves a value judgment about the societies to which the concept is applied. Thus, the evaluation immediately destroys the objectivity that is its sole claim. The same prejudice – for finally it is that – perverts and dooms the attempt to evaluate political power in these societies. That is, the model to which political power is referred and the unit by which it is measured are constituted *in advance* by the idea Western civilization has shaped and developed. From its beginnings our culture has conceived of political power in terms of hierarchized and authoritarian relations of command and obedience. Every real or possible form of power is consequently reducible to this privileged relation which a priori expresses the essence of power. If the reduction is not possible it is because one is on this side of the political, so that the absence of any command-obedience relationship ipso facto entails the absence of political power. Hence, there exist not only societies without a state, but also societies without power. The still robust adversary was recognized long ago, the obstacle constantly blocking anthropological research: the ethnocentrism that mediates all attention directed to differences in order to reduce them to identity and finally to suppress them. There

4. Clastres's emphasis.

exists a kind of ethnological ritual that consists in exposing the risks of this attitude. The intention is laudable, but it does not always prevent ethnologists from succumbing more or less inadvertently to this attitude in turn, with more or less untroubled minds. It is true, as Lapierre has justifiably emphasized, that ethnocentrism is the most widely shared thing in the world. Every culture is, one might say, by definition ethnocentric in its narcissistic relationship with itself. However, a considerable difference separates Western ethnocentrism from its "primitive" counterpart. The savage belonging to some Indian or Australian tribe deems his culture superior to all others without feeling obliged to deliver a scientific discourse about them. Ethnology, on the other hand, wants to situate itself directly within the realm of universality without realizing that in many respects it remains firmly entrenched in its particularity, and that its pseudo-scientific discourse quickly deteriorates into genuine ideology. (Some assertions to the effect that only Western civilization is able to produce ethnologists are thereby reduced to their true significance.) It is not a scientific proposition to determine that some cultures lack political power because they show nothing similar to what is found in our culture. It is instead the sign of a certain conceptual poverty.

Ethnocentrism is not, therefore, a negligible hindrance to reflection, and the importance of its implications is greater than one might think. It cannot permit differences to remain, each one for itself in its neutrality, but insists on comprehending them as differences measured in terms of what is most familiar, power as it is experienced and conceived of in the culture of the West. Ethnocentrism's old accomplice, evolutionism, is not far off. At this level, the approach is twofold: first make an inventory of societies according to the greater or lesser proximity their type of power has to ours; then assert explicitly (as in the past) or implicitly (as at present) a *continuity* between these various forms of power.

Because anthropology, following Lowie's example, has rejected the tenets of Morgan and Engels as simplistic, it is no longer able (at least where the political question is at issue) to express itself in sociological terms. But since, on the other hand, the temptation to continue thinking along the same lines is too strong, *biological* metaphors are invoked. Whence the vocabulary noted above: embryonic, nascent, poorly developed, etc. Scarcely a half-century ago the perfect model all cultures tried to achieve through the historical process was the Western adult male – educated and of sound mind (perhaps a Ph.D. in the physical sciences). Such a thing is still imagined no doubt, but it is no longer said. Yet, if the language has changed, the discourse has not. For what is an embryonic power, if not that which could and should *develop* to the adult state? And what is this adult state whose embryonic beginnings are discovered here and there? It is none other than the type of power to which the ethnologist is accustomed – that belonging to the culture which produces ethnologists, the West. And why are those cultural fetuses always destined to perish? How does it happen that the societies which conceive them abort so frequently? Obviously, this congenital frailty is attributable to their archaism, their underdevelopment, to the fact that they are not the West. Archaic societies would thus be sociological axolotls, incapable of reaching the normal adult state without external aid.

The biologism of this mode of expression is clearly no more than the furtive mask hiding the ancient Western conviction – a conviction indeed often shared by ethnology, or at least by many of its practitioners – that history is a one-way street, that societies without power are the image of what we have ceased to be, and that for them our culture is the image of what they have to become. And not only is our system of power considered the best, the archaic societies are even made party to a similar persuasion. For to declare that "no Nilotic people has been able to rise to the centralized level of the political organizations of the great Bantu kingdoms," or that "Lobi society has been unable to create a political organization" is to assert, in a sense, that these peoples have undertaken to provide themselves with a *true* political power. What reason could there be for saying that the Sioux Indians have failed to achieve something attained by the Aztecs, or that the Bororo have been incapable of raising themselves to the political level of the Incas? The archeology of anthropological language would lead us to uncover a secret kinship between ideology and ethnology. And without the need for much digging, since the ground is finally rather thin; as a matter of fact, if care is not taken ethnology is destined to splash about in the same quagmire as sociology and psychology.

Is a political anthropology possible? That is doubtful when one considers the still growing stream of literature devoted to the problem of power. What is especially striking in this literature is the gradual dissolution of the political. Failing to find it where they expected, the authors believe they have located it at every level of archaic societies, with the result that everything falls within the bounds of the political. All the sub-groups and units (kinship groups, age groups, production units, and so forth) that make up a society are haphazardly endowed with a political significance which eventually covers the whole social sphere and consequently loses its specific character. For if political reality is found everywhere, it is found nowhere. Which makes one wonder, for that matter, whether they are trying to say precisely *that*, i.e., archaic societies are not authentic societies because they are not political societies. In short, the ethnographer would be justified in proclaiming that political power is inconceivable in these societies, since he annihilates it in the very act of grasping it. Nothing, however, precludes the assumption that ethnology only raises problems it can solve. So it is necessary to ask: what conditions must obtain before political power becomes conceivable? If anthropology is going nowhere, the reason is because it has come to a dead end and needs, therefore, to change course. The road on which it has gone astray is the easiest, the one that can be followed blindly; the one mapped out by our own cultural world; not insofar as it unfolds within the universal, but rather insofar as it shows itself to be just as limited as any other. The necessary condition is to abandon – ascetically, as it were – the *exotic* conception of the archaic world, a conception which, in the last analysis, overwhelmingly characterizes allegedly scientific discourse regarding that world. This implies the decision to take *seriously*, at last, the men and women who live in primitive societies, from every viewpoint and in all their dimensions: the political dimension included, even and especially when the latter is experienced in archaic societies as the negation of its opposite number in the Western world. It is imperative to accept the idea that negation does not signify nothingness; that when the mirror does not reflect our own likeness, it does not prove there is nothing to perceive. More simply: just as our culture finally recognized that primitive man is not a child but, individually, an adult, in the same manner it will mark a slight progress when it comes to acknowledge his collective maturity as well.

Therefore, peoples without a writing system are no less adult than literate societies. Their history has the same depth as ours and, short of racism, there is no reason to judge them incapable of reflecting on their experience and of discovering the appropriate solutions to their problems. Indeed that is why it will not do to state that in those societies in which the command-obedience relation is unknown (that is, in societies devoid of political power), the life of the group is maintained through *immediate social control*, adding at once that this control is *apolitical*. What exactly is meant by such a statement? What is the political referent that makes it possible, by contrast, to speak of the apolitical? But, to be precise, there is nothing political since we are dealing with societies without power: how then can one speak of the apolitical? Either the political is present, even in those societies, or the expression immediate social control is self-contradictory and in any case tautological. In fact, what do we learn from it concerning the societies to which it is applied? And how exacting is Lowie's explanation, for instance, according to which, in societies without power, there exists "an unofficial power of public opinion"? It was remarked that if everything is political, then nothing is: but if somewhere there exists something that can be called apolitical, this means that elsewhere there is something political! Logically speaking, an apolitical society would no longer have a place within the sphere of culture, but would rightly be placed among animal societies governed by natural relations of domination and submission.

Here we have perhaps the main obstacle for classical thought regarding power: it is impossible to think the apolitical without the political, immediate social control without the concept of mediation – in a word, *society without power*. Hopefully, it has been shown that the epistemological obstacle that "politicology" has thus far been unable to overcome lies within the cultural ethnocentrism of Western thought, itself linked to an exotic view of non-Western societies. If ethnographers persist in reflecting on power, starting from the assurance that its true form has been realized in our culture, and if they continue to make this form the measure of all the others, even of their telos, then discursive consistency will be abandoned, and the science will be allowed to degenerate into opinion. Perhaps there is no need for the science of man. But given the determination to establish it and to articulate the ethnological discourse, it is appropriate to show archaic cultures a little respect and to ask oneself about the validity of such categories as subsistence economy or immediate social control. If this critical task is not performed, one is in danger first of letting the social reality escape one's grasp, then of misdirecting the empirical description itself. In this way, depending on the societies observed and on the imagination of the observer, one ends by finding something political everywhere or by finding it nowhere at all.

We believe the previously cited example of Amerindian societies illustrates quite well the impossibility of speaking of societies without political power. This is not the place to define the status of the political in this type of culture. We shall go no further than to reject what ethnocentrists take for granted: that the bounds of power are set by coercion, beyond which and short of which no power would exist. In fact, power exists (not only in America but in many other primitive cultures) totally separate from violence and apart from any hierarchy. Consequently, all societies, whether archaic or not, are political, even if the political is expressed in many voices, even if their meaning is not immediately decipherable, and even if one has to solve the riddle of a "powerless" power. This leads to a number of conclusions:

(1) Societies cannot be divided into two groups: societies with power and societies without power. On the contrary, it is our view (in complete conformity with ethnographic data) that political power is *universal*, immanent to social reality (whether the social is defined by "blood ties" or social classes); and that it manifests itself in two primary modes: coercive power, and non-coercive power.

(2) Political power as coercion (or as the relation of command-obedience) is not the *only* model of true power, but simply a *particular case*, a concrete realization of political power in some cultures, Western culture for instance (but, of course, the latter is not the only instance). Hence, there is no scientific reason for granting that modality the privilege of serving as the reference point and the basis for explaining other and different modalities.

(3) Even in societies in which the political institution is absent, where for example chiefs do not exist, *even there* the political is

present, even there the question of power is posed: not in the misleading sense of wanting to account for an impossible absence, but in the contrary sense whereby, perhaps mysteriously, *something exists within the absence.* If political power is not a necessity inherent in human nature, i.e., in man as a natural being (and there Nietzsche is wrong), it is a necessity inherent in social life. The political can be conceived apart from violence; the social cannot be conceived without the political. In other words, there are no societies without power. This is why we can employ for our own purposes, in certain respects, B. de Jouvenel's formulation: "It has become apparent that authority is what creates the social bond," and simultaneously subscribe fully to Lapierre's criticism of it. For if, as we believe, the political is at the very heart of the social, it cannot be understood in de Jouvenel's terms. For him the political apparently boils down to "the personal influence" of strong individuals. It is not possible to be more naively (but is it really a matter of naiveté?) ethnocentric.

The above remarks open a perspective in which to situate the theory which Lapierre argues throughout the fourth section of his book: "Political power derives from social innovation" (p. 529), and again: "Political power develops the more readily as social innovation becomes more important, its rhythm more intense, its scope more wide-ranging" (p. 621). The author's demonstration, supported as it is by numerous examples, seems rigorous and convincing, and we can only affirm our agreement with his analyses and conclusions. With one reservation, however: the political power involved, the type deriving from social innovation, is the power we call coercive. What we mean is that Lapierre's theory is concerned with societies in which the command-obedience relation is observed, but not with the others: Indian societies, for example, cannot be thought of as societies in which political power derives from social innovation. In other words, social innovation is perhaps the basis of coercive political power, but it is certainly not the basis of non-coercive power, unless it is decided (something impossible) that only coercive power exists. The range of Lapierre's theory is limited to a certain type of society, a specific mode of political power, since it means implicitly that where there is no social innovation, there is no political power. It contributes a valuable insight nonetheless: viz., that political power as coercion or violence is the stamp of *historical* societies, that is, societies which bear within them the cause of innovation, change, and historicity. Thus it would be possible to order the various societies along a new axis: societies with non-coercive political power are societies without history, societies with coercive political power are historical societies. An arrangement quite different from that implied by current thinking about power, which equates societies without history to societies without power.

Innovation is therefore the basis of coercion, not the political. It follows that Lapierre's work completes only half the program, since the question of the basis of non-coercive power is not addressed. It is a question that can be posed more succinctly, and in a more acute form: why is there such a thing as political power? Why is there political power rather than nothing? We do not claim to furnish the answer; our aim has been merely to state why previous answers are unsatisfactory and on what condition a correct answer is possible. This is the same as defining the task of a general, not a regional, political anthropology, a task that divides into two major lines of inquiry:

(1) What is political power? That is: what is society? (2) What explains the transition from non-coercive political power to coercive political power, and how does the transition come about? That is: what is history?

We will restrict ourselves to the observation that Marx and Engels, despite their considerable ethnological background, never committed their thought to this path, assuming that they ever clearly formulated the question. Lapierre notes that "the truth of Marxism is that there would be no political power if there had not been conflicts between social forces." It is a truth no doubt, but one valid only for societies where social forces are in conflict. That power cannot be understood as violence (and its ultimate form: the centralized state) without social conflict is beyond argument. But what of societies without conflict, those in which "primitive communism" obtains? And is Marxism able to account for this transition from non-history to historicity and from non-coercion to violence? If it were, it would in fact be a universal theory of society and history, and therefore would be anthropology. What was the first motor of social change? Perhaps we should look for it in the very thing that in archaic societies is concealed from our gaze, *in the political itself*. It thus would be necessary to return to Durkheim's idea (or set it back on its feet), according to which political power presupposes social differentiation: might it not be political power that constitutes society's absolute difference? Could that not be the radical fissure at the root of the social, the initial break on which all movement and all history depend, the primal splitting at the core of all differences?

A Copernican revolution is at stake, in the sense that in some respects, ethnology until now has let primitive cultures revolve around Western civilization in a centripetal motion, so to speak. Political anthropology appears to have made it abundantly clear that a complete reversal of perspectives is necessary (insofar as there is the desire to engage in a discourse concerning archaic societies that conforms to their reality and not ours). Political anthropology encounters a limit that is not so much a property of primitive societies as it is something carried within anthropology itself, the limitation of the West itself, whose seal is still engraved upon it. In order to escape the attraction of its native earth and attain real freedom of thought, in order to pull itself away from the facts of natural history in which it continues to flounder, reflection on power must effect a "heliocentric" conversion: it will then perhaps succeed in better understanding the world of others, and consequently our own. The path of its conversion is shown, moreover, by a contemporary mind which has been able to take seriously that of Savages: the work of Claude Lévi-Strauss proves to us the soundness of this approach by the wealth of its accomplishments (these are perhaps still not fully recognized) and invites us to go farther. It is time to change suns, time to move on.

Lapierre begins his work by denouncing, rightly, a claim shared by the social sciences: they believe they can insure their scientific status by breaking all links to what they call philosophy. Of course, there is hardly any need for such a reference in order to describe calabashes or kinship systems. But something very different is involved, and it is to be feared that, under the alias of philosophy, it is simply *thought* itself they are trying to expel. Does this mean, then, that science and thought are mutually exclusive: that science is constructed from non-thought, or even anti-thought? The nonsense – sometimes mild, sometimes abrasive – uttered from all sides by the militants of "science" seems to lean in that direction. But in this instance one must be able to recognize where this frantic inclination to anti-thought leads: under the cover of "science," of epigonal platitudes, or less simple-minded endeavors, it leads straight to obscurantism.

This is a cheerless idea to ponder, discouraging to any *gaya scienza*: if it is less tiring to descend than it is to climb, is it not true, however, that thought is loyal to itself only when it moves *against the incline*?

Exchange and Power

Ethnological theory oscillates, therefore, between two opposing and yet complementary ideas of political power: for the first, primitive societies in the main are devoid of real political organization. The absence of any visible and effective organ of power has led some to deny these societies even the function of power. They are considered as stagnating in a pre-political or anarchic historical stage. For the second, a minority of primitive societies has transcended primordial anarchy and attained the only form of authentically human group existence: the political institution.

But the "lack" that characterizes the majority of societies is converted in the contrary case into "excess," and the institution perverted into despotism or tyranny. It is as if primitive societies faced the alternative: either the lack of the institution and anarchy, or an excess of this same institution and despotism. But this seeming alternative is really a dilemma: the true political condition always evades primitive man. It is this all but inescapable failure to which early ethnology naively condemned primitive man that reveals the complementarity of the extremes. Both agree in denying him the "right measure" of political power: one by deficiency, the other by excess.

In this respect South America offers a quite remarkable example of the tendency to place primitive societies within the framework of this dualistic macro-typology. The anarchic separatism of the majority of Indian societies is contrasted to the massive nature of the Inca organization, "the totalitarian empire of the past." Yet, given their political organization, most Indian societies of America are distinguished by their sense of democracy and taste for equality. The first explorers of Brazil and the ethnographers who came after often emphasized the fact that the most notable characteristic of the Indian chief consists of his almost complete lack of authority; among these people the political function appears barely differentiated. Though it is scattered and inadequate, the documentation we have lends support to that vivid impression of democracy common to all those who studied American societies. Among the great number of tribes accounted for in South America, the authority of the chieftaincy is explicitly documented only in the case of a few groups, such as the island Taino, the Caquetio, the Jirajira, and the Otomac. But it should be pointed out that these groups, almost all of whom are Arawak, are located in the northwestern part of South America and that their social organization presents a marked stratification into castes: this latter feature is found again only among the Guaycuru and Arawak (Guana) tribes of the Chaco. One can further assume that the societies of the Northwest are bound to a cultural tradition closer to the Chibcha civilization and the Andean region than to those referred to as Tropical Forest cultures. It is the lack of social stratification and the authority of power that should be stressed as the distinguishing features of the political organization of the majority of Indian societies. Some of them, such as the Ona and the Yahgan of Tierra del Fuego, do not even possess the institution of chieftainship; and it is said of the Jivaro that their language has no term for the chief.

To a mind shaped by cultures in which political power is endowed with real might, the distinctive rule of the American chieftainship is asserted in paradoxical fashion. Just what is this power that is deprived of its own exercise? What is it that defines the chief, since he lacks authority? And one might soon be tempted, yielding to the temptation of a more or less conscious evolutionism, to conclude that political power in these societies is epiphenomenal, that their archaism prevents them from creating a genuine political form. However, to solve the problem in this fashion compels one to frame it again in a different way: from where does this institution without "substance" derive its strength to endure? For what needs to be understood is the bizarre persistence of a "power" that is practically powerless, of a chieftainship without authority, of a function operating in a void.

In a text written in 1948, R. Lowie, analyzing the distinctive features of the type of chief alluded to above, labeled by him *titular chief*, isolates three essential traits of the Indian leader. These traits recur throughout the two Americas, making it possible to grasp them as the necessary conditions of power in those areas:

(1) The chief is a "peacemaker"; he is the group's moderating agency, a fact borne out by the frequent division of power into civil and military.

(2) He must be generous with his possessions, and cannot allow himself, without betraying his office, to reject the incessant demands of those under his "administration."

(3) Only a good orator can become chief.

This pattern of triple qualification indispensable to the holder of the political office is, in all probability, equally valid for both North and South American societies. First of all, it is truly remarkable that the features of the chieftainship stand in strong contrast to one another in time of war and in time of peace. Quite often the leadership of the group is assumed by two different individuals. Among the Cubeo, for instance, or among the tribes of the Orinoco, there exists a civil power and a military power. During military expeditions the war chief commands a substantial amount of power – at times absolute – over the group of warriors. But once peace is restored the war chief loses all his power. The model of coercive power is adopted, therefore, only in exceptional circumstances when the group faces an external threat. But the conjunction of power and coercion ends as soon as the group returns to its normal internal life. Thus, the authority of Tupinamba chiefs, unchallenged during war expeditions, was closely supervised by the council of elders during peacetime. Similarly, the Jivaro are reported to have a chief only in time of war. Normal civil power, based on the *consensus omnium* and not on constraint, is thus profoundly peaceful and its function is "pacification": the chief is responsible for maintaining peace and harmony in the group. He must appease quarrels and settle disputes – not by employing a force he does not possess and which would not be acknowledged in any case, but by relying solely on the strength of his prestige, his fairness, and his verbal ability. More than a judge who passes sentence, he is an arbiter who seeks to reconcile. The chief can do nothing to prevent a dispute from turning into a feud if he fails to effect a reconciliation of the contending parties. That plainly reveals the disjunction between power and coercion.

The second characteristic of the Indian chieftainship – generosity – appears to be more than a duty: it is a bondage. Ethnologists have observed that among the most varied peoples of South America this obligation to give, to which the chief is bound, is experienced by the Indians as a kind of right to subject him to a continuous looting. And if the unfortunate leader tries to check this flight of gifts, he is immediately shorn of all prestige and power. Francis Huxley writes of the Urubu: "It is the business of a chief to be generous and to give what is asked of him. In some Indian tribes you can always tell the chief because he has the fewest posses-

able to find sound reasons for accepting it – reasons we must try to elucidate.

It is interesting to examine the ethnographic material on this subject despite its many gaps: our information about many tribes is very meager and in some cases all that is known about a tribe is its name. However, it seems possible to grant certain recurrent phenomena statistical probability. Keeping in mind the approximate but probable figure of about 200 ethnic groups for all of South America, one realizes that the information available on them attests to the existence of strict monogamy only for some ten groups: these are, for example, the Palicur of Guiana, the Apinayé and the Timbira of the Gé group, and the Yagua of the Northern Amazon. Without assigning to these calculations a precision they certainly do not possess, they are nonetheless indicative of an order of magnitude: scarcely one-twentieth of these societies practices strict monogamy. That is, most of the groups recognize polygyny and the extension of the latter is virtually continental.

But it should also be mentioned that Indian polygyny is limited strictly to a small number of individuals, nearly always chiefs. And it is understandable that the situation could not be otherwise. If one takes into account the fact that the natural sex ratio, or numerical relationship of the sexes, could never be such as to permit every man to marry more than one woman, it is obvious that generalized polygyny is a biological impossibility: hence, it is culturally restricted to certain individuals. This natural determination is confirmed by an examination of the ethnographic data: of the 180 or 190 tribes practicing polygyny, only ten or so do not assign it any limits. That is, in those tribes every adult male can marry more than one woman. They are, for example, the Achagua, who are northwestern Arawak, the Chibcha, the Jivaro, and the Rucuyen, a Carib people of Guiana.

The Achagua and Chibcha, belonging to the cultural area called the Circum-Caribbean, whose boundaries fall within Venezuela and Colombia, were very different from the rest of the South American peoples. Caught up in a process of extreme social stratification, they reduced their less powerful neighbors to slavery and thus benefitted from a steady and substantial supply of women prisoners, whom they took at once as supplementary wives. As for the Jivaro, their passion for war and headhunting in all probability entailed a very high mortality rate for the young warriors. This, in turn, allowed most of the men to practice polygyny. The Rucuyen, along with several other Carib groups of Venezuela, were also a very bellicose people: most of the time their military expeditions aimed at procuring slaves and secondary wives.

All the foregoing shows, first, the naturally determined rarity of generalized polygyny. Secondly, when it is not restricted to the chief, it is due to cultural factors: the existence of castes, the practice of slavery, and the pursuit of war. On the face of it, these latter societies seem more democratic than the others. Polygyny, as they practice it, has ceased to be the privilege of a single individual. And in fact the contrast seems more clear-cut between an Iquito chief, who may possess a dozen women, and the men under him who are tied down to monogamy, than between an Achagua chief and the men of his group for whom polygyny is equally permitted.

Let us recall, however, that the societies of the Northwest were already highly stratified. An aristocracy of rich nobles, by virtue of its wealth, commanded the means to be more polygynous – if it can be so phrased – than the less fortunate "plebians": the model of marriage by purchase permitted the rich men to acquire a larger number of wives. So that between polygyny as the privilege of the chief and generalized polygyny, the difference is not in kind but degree: a Chibcha or Achagua plebian could scarcely marry more than two or three woman, while a famous chief from the Northwest – Guaramental – had 200.

Given the preceding analysis, it is legitimate to assume that for most South American societies the matrimonial institution of polygyny is closely linked to the political institution of power. The specific character of this link would be negated only by the restoration of the conditions for monogamy: a polygyny extended equally to all men of the group. Now, a brief look at a few societies possessing the generalized model of plural marriage reveals that the contrast between the chief and the rest of the men is maintained and even reinforced.

Because they were invested with real power, certain Tupinamba warriors – the most successful in combat – could have secondary wives, often prisoners wrested from the defeated group. And the "Council," to which the chief was compelled to submit all decisions, was in part composed precisely of the most outstanding warriors. It was generally from the latter that the assembly of men chose the new chief when the dead leader's son was deemed unworthy of the office. Further, if some groups recognize polygyny as the privilege of the best hunters as well as the chief, this is because hunting – as an economic activity and an activity involving prestige – assumes a special importance sanctioned by the influence conferred on the skillful man by his adroitness in bringing back a lot of game.

Among such peoples as the Pur-Coroado, the Caingang, or the Ipurina of the Jurua-Purus, hunting is a critical source of food. Accordingly, the best hunters acquire a social status and political "weight" consonant with their professional merits. The leader's main task being to safeguard his group's welfare, the Ipurina or Caingang chief will be one of the best hunters. And it is the latter who generally provide the men eligible for the chieftainship.

Not only is a good hunter in a position to supply the needs of a polygynous family. Hunting is an activity essential to the survival of the group. This guarantees the political importance of those men who are most successful at it. By permitting the most effective food providers to practice polygyny, the group – taking out a mortgage on the future, so to speak – implicitly acknowledges their quality as potential leaders. But attention must be called to the fact that this polygyny, far from being egalitarian, always favors the actual chief of the group.

The polygynic model of marriage, viewed in its various extensions: general or restricted, restricted either to the chief alone or to the chief and a small minority of men, has consistently referred us back to the political life of the group; this is the horizon on which polygyny traces its pattern, and perhaps this is the place where the meaning of its function can be read.

It is surely by four traits that the chief is distinguished in South America. As chief, he is a "professional pacifier"; in addition, he has to be generous and a good orator; finally, polygyny is his prerogative.

A distinction is called for, however, between the first of these criteria and the following three. The latter define the set of prestations and counter-prestations which maintain the balance between the social structure and the political institution: the leader exercises a right over an abnormal number of the group's women; in return, the group is justified in requiring of its chief generosity and talent as a speaker. This relation, apparently in the category of exchange, is thus determined at an essential level of society, a sociological level, properly speaking, that concerns the very social structure of the group as such. In contrast, the moderating function of the chief operates in the different element of strictly political practice. In fact, one cannot situate on the same sociological plane, as Lowie appears to do, the conclusions contained in the preceding analysis: (1) the set of conditions defining the possibility of the political sphere; (2) the effective implementation – experienced as such – which constitutes the everyday function of the institution. To treat as homogenous elements the mode in which power is constituted, and constituted power's mode of performance would, in effect, lead one to confuse the *nature* of chieftainship with its *activity*, the transcendental with the empirical aspect of the institution.

Humble in scope, the chief's functions are controlled nonetheless by public opinion. A planner of the group's economic and ceremonial activities, the leader possesses no decision-making power; he is never certain that his "orders" will be carried out. This permanent fragility of a power unceasingly contested imparts its *tonality* to the exercise of the office: the power of the chief depends on the good will of the group. It thus becomes easy to understand the direct interest the chief has in maintaining peace: the outbreak of a crisis that would destroy internal harmony calls for the intervention of power, but simultaneously gives rise to that *intention* to contest which the chief has not the means to overcome.

The function, by being exercised, thus points to the thing whose meaning we are seeking: the impotence of the institution. But this meaning exists, disguised, on the structural plane, that is, on another level. As the concrete activity of the function, the chief's practice does not refer, therefore, to the same order of phenomena as the other three criteria; it lets them stand as a unity structurally linked to the very essence of society.

In fact, it is extraordinary to discover that this trinity of predicates – oratorical talent, generosity, and polygyny – attached to the person of the leader, concerns the same elements whose exchange and circulation constitute society as such and sanctions the transition from nature to culture. Society is defined primarily by the three fundamental levels of the exchange of goods, women, and words; and it is equally by direct reference to these three types of "signs" that the political sphere of Indian societies is constituted. Hence, power relates here (if this concurrence is to be considered more than an insignificant coincidence) to the three essential structural levels of society; that is, it is at the very heart of the communicative universe. We next need to try and clarify the nature of this relationship so as to draw out its structural implications.

Apparently, power is faithful to the law of exchange which founds and regulates society; it seems as if the chief received a part of the group's women in exchange for economic goods and linguistic signs, the only difference resulting from the fact that here the exchange-units are, on one hand, an individual and, on the other, the group as a whole. However, such an interpretation, based on the impression that the principle of reciprocity determines the relationship between power and society, is soon found lacking: we know that the Indian societies of South America as a rule possess only a rudimentary technology, and that, consequently, no individual, including the chief, is capable of amassing very much material wealth. As we have seen, the prestige of a chief is due in large part to his generosity. But the expectations of the Indians quite often exceed the immediate possibilities of the chief. He is forced therefore, under penalty of seeing himself rapidly forsaken by most of his people, to try to satisfy their demands. No doubt his wives are able in large measure to support him in his job: the example of the Nambikwara well illustrates the crucial role of the chief's wives. But some objects – bows, arrows, masculine ornaments – which the hunters and warriors are fond of can only be manufactured by their chief; now his productive capacity is greatly limited, and that of necessity limits the range of prestations in goods from the chief to the group. We also know in this connection that for primitive societies women are consummate values. In that case, how is it possible to claim that this apparent exchange brings into play two equivalent "quantities" of value, an equivalence that should be expected, however, if the principle of reciprocity indeed works to link society to its form of power? It is evident that for the group, which has relinquished a considerable quantity of its most essential values – the women – for the chief's benefit, the daily harangues and the meager economic goods of which the leader disposes do not amount to an equivalent compensation. And this is even less the case as, despite his lack of authority, the chief enjoys an enviable social status. The unequal character of the "exchange" is striking: it would make sense only in societies where power, equipped with effective authority, would by that very fact be sharply differentiated from the rest of the group. Now it is precisely this authority which the Indian chief lacks: how then interpret the fact that an office rewarded with exorbitant privileges is yet powerless in its exercise?

By analyzing the relationship between power and the group in terms of exchange, one brings into sharper focus the paradox of this relationship. Let us consider, therefore, the status of each of these three levels of communication, taken separately, at the center of the political sphere. It is obvious that as regards the women, their circulation occurs in "one-way" fashion – from the group towards the chief; for the latter would be clearly incapable of placing back into the circuit, in the direction of the group, a number of women equal to that which he has received from it. Of course, the chief's wives will give him daughters who later will be as many potential wives for the young men of the group. But it should not be thought that the daughter's reinsertion into the cycle of matrimonial exchanges serves to compensate for the father's polygyny. In reality, in most South American societies, the chieftainship is inherited patrilineally. Thus, making allowance for individual aptitudes, the chief's son, or, failing that, the son of the chief's brother, will be the new leader of the community. And along with the responsibility, he will garner the privilege of the office, namely polygyny. Hence the exercise of this privilege cancels, with each new generation, the effect of the thing that might have neutralized, by way of the women, the polygyny of the previous generation. It is not on the diachronic plane of succeeding generations that the drama of power is acted out, but rather on the synchronic plane of the structure of the group. The advent of a chief reproduces the same situation each time; this structure of repetition would come to an end only from the cyclical standpoint of a power that would pass round to all the families of the group in succession, the chief being chosen every generation from a different family, until the first family is arrived at once more, thus commencing a new cycle. But the job is hereditary: here it is not a matter of exchange, therefore, but of a pure and simple gift from the group to its leader, a gift with no reciprocation, apparently meant to sanction the social status of the holder of a responsibility established for the purpose of not being exercised.

If we turn to the economic level of exchange, we notice that goods are subjected to the same treatment: their movement is effected solely from the chief to the group. The Indian societies of South America are in fact rarely bound to make economic prestations to their leader, and he has to cultivate his manioc and kill his own game like everybody else. With the exception of certain societies of the northwestern part of South America, the privileges of chieftainship are generally not situated on the material plane, and only a few tribes make idleness into the mark of a superior social status: the Manasi of Bolivia and the Guarani work the chief's gardens and harvest his crops. It should be remarked in addition that among the Guarani the use of this right favors the chief perhaps less than the shaman. However that may be, the majority of Indian leaders hardly project the image of a do-nothing king: quite the contrary, the chief, obliged as he is to respond with expected generosity, must constantly think of ways to obtain gifts to offer to his people. Barter with other groups can be a source of goods; but more often the chief has to rely on his own ingenuity and labor. Curiously enough, in South America it is the leader who works the hardest.

Lastly, the status of linguistic signs is more evident still: in societies that have been able to protect their language from the degradation visited on it by our own, speaking is more than a privilege, it is a duty of the chief. It is to him that the mastery of words falls, to such an extent that someone was able to write, on the subject of a North American tribe: "It can be said not that the chief is a man who speaks, but that he who speaks is a chief," a statement easily applicable to the whole South American continent. The exercise of this near-monopoly over language is further reinforced by the fact that Indians do not perceive the situation as a frustration. The demarcation is so clearly established that the Trumai leader's two assistants, for instance, although they benefit from a certain prestige, cannot *speak* like the chief: not by virtue of an external prohibition, but because of the feeling that the speaking activity would be an insult both to the chief and to the language; for – says an informant – anyone other than the chief "would be ashamed" to speak as he does.

In rejecting the notion of an exchange of the women of the group against the goods and messages of the chief, we consequently turn to examine the movement of each "sign" according to its particular circuit and discover that this triple movement manifests a common negative dimension which assigns these three types of "signs" an identical fate: they no longer appear as exchange values, reciprocity ceases to regulate their circulation, and each of them falls, therefore, outside the province of communication. Hence a new relationship between the domain of power and the essence of the group now comes to light: power enjoys a privileged relationship toward those elements whose reciprocal movement founds the very structure of society. But this relationship, by denying these elements an exchange value at the group level, institutes the political sphere not only as external to the structure of the group, but further still, as negating that structure: power is contrary to the group, and the rejection of reciprocity, as the ontological dimension of society, is the rejection of society itself.

Such a conclusion, joined to the premise of the powerlessness of the chief in Indian societies, may seem paradoxical; it is this conclusion, however, that holds the key to the initial problem: the chieftainship's lack of authority. In fact, in order for one aspect of the social structure to be able to exert any influence on this structure, it is necessary, at the very least, that the relationship between the particular system and the total system be other than entirely negative. The effective elaboration of the political function is possible only if it is in some way inherent in the group. Now in Indian societies this function is excluded from the group, and is even exclusive of the latter: hence it is in the negative relation maintained with regard to the group that the impotence of the political function is rooted. The ejection of the political function from society is the very means of reducing it to impotence.

To thus conceive the relationship between power and society among the Indian peoples of South America may seem to imply a teleological metaphysics, according to which some mysterious will would employ devious means so as to deprive political power of precisely its quality as power. It is not at all a matter of final causes, however. The phenomena analyzed here belong to the field of unconscious activity by means of which the group fashions its models: and it is the structural model of the relation of the social group to political power that we are trying to uncover. This model allows us to integrate data initially perceived as contradictory. At this stage of analysis, we can see that the impotence of power is tied directly to its "marginal" position in relation to the total system; and this position itself results from the rupture that power injects into the decisive cycle of the exchange of women, goods, and words. But to detect in this rupture the *cause* of the powerlessness of the political function still throws no light on its profound *reason for being*. Ought the sequence: rupture of exchange-externality-impotence, be interpreted as an accidental detour of the process that constitutes power? That would allow one to suppose that the *result* of the operation (power's lack of authority) is merely contingent with respect to the initial *intention* (the promotion of the political sphere). But it would then be necessary to accept the idea that this "error" is coextensive with the model itself and that it is repeated indefinitely across a nearly continental area: in this way, none of the cultures that inhabit the area would prove capable of providing themselves with a genuine political authority. It would also mean accepting the underlying postulate – totally arbitrary – that these cultures do not possess any creativity: at the same time it would be a return to the presumption of their archaism. Hence it is not possible to conceive of the separation between the political function and authority as the accidental failure of a process aiming at their synthesis, as the "skidding" of a system unwittingly confounded by a result which the group would be incapable of correcting.

Challenging the viewpoint of the accident leads us to assume a certain necessity inherent in the process itself, and to seek the ultimate *reason* for the result at the level of sociological *intentionality*, this being the place where the model takes form. To grant that the result conforms to the intention that presided over its production can only signify that this result was implied in the original intention: power is exactly what these societies intended it to be. And as this power is – to put it schematically – nothing, the group thereby reveals its radical rejection of authority, an utter negation of power. Is it possible to account for this "decision" by Indian cultures? Must we decide that it is the irrational outcome of fantasy, or can we, on the contrary, postulate a rationality immanent to this "choice"? The very radical character of the refusal, its persistence and extension, perhaps suggests the perspective in which to place it. The relationship between power and exchange, although negative, has nonetheless shown that it is at the deepest level of the social structure: the site of the unconscious constitution of its dimensions, where the problematic of power arises and takes shape. Stating it differently, it is culture itself, as nature's absolute difference, that becomes totally invested in the rejection of this power. And is it not precisely in its relation to nature that culture manifests a repudiation of equal profundity? The identical character of the two instances of rejection brings us to discern in these societies an identification of power with nature: culture is the negation of both, not in the sense that power and nature would be two different dangers, the sameness of which would be that of an identical – negative – relationship to a third term, but indeed in the sense that culture apprehends power as the very resurgence of nature.

In fact, it is as though these societies formed their political sphere in terms of an intuition which for them would take the place of a rule: namely, that power is essentially coercion; that the unifying activity of the political function would be performed not on the basis of the structure of society and in conformity with it, but on the basis of an uncontrollable and antagonistic beyond; that in essence power is no more than the furtive manifestation of nature in *its* power. Hence, far from giving us the lackluster image of an inability to resolve the question of political power, these societies astonish us by the subtlety with which they have posed and settled the question. They had a very early premonition that power's transcendence conceals a mortal risk for the group, that the principle of an authority which is external and the creator of its own legality is a challenge to culture itself. It is the intuition of this threat that determined the depth of their political philosophy. For, on discovering the great affinity of power and nature, as the twofold limitation of the domain of culture, Indian societies were able to create a means for neutralizing the virulence of political authority. They chose themselves to be the founders of that authority, but in such a manner as to let power appear only as a negativity that is immediately subdued: they established it in keeping with its essence (the negation of culture), but precisely in order to strip it of any real might. Thus, the advent of power, such as it is, presents itself to these societies as the very means for nullifying that power. The same operation that institutes the political sphere forbids it the exercise of its jurisdiction: it is in this manner that culture uses against power the very ruse of nature. That is why the one called chief is the man in whom the exchange of women, words, and goods shatters.

As the purveyor of wealth and messages, the chief conveys nothing but his dependence on the group, and the obligation to exhibit at every moment the innocence of his office. Yet, it might seem that in the confidence the group places in its chief, a freedom experienced by the group in its dealings with power, there is the surreptitious hint of control by the chief over the community – a control that runs deeper for being less apparent. For in certain circumstances, in particular during a period of scarcity, the group places itself entirely in the hands of the chief; when famine threatens, the communities of the Orinoco install themselves in the chief's house, deciding to live at his expense until better days return. Similarly, the Nambikwara band, after a long spell of food shortage, looks to the chief and not to itself to improve the situation. It seems in this case that the group, unable to do without the chief, wholly depends on him. But this subordination is merely apparent: it actually masks a kind of blackmail the group uses against the chief. For if the latter does not do what is expected of him, his village or band will simply abandon him and throw in with a leader more faithful in his duties. It is only on condition of this real dependence that the chief can keep his status.

It appears very clearly in the relationship between power and the spoken word: for if language is the very opposite of violence, speech must be interpreted as more than the privilege of the chief; as the means the group provides itself with to maintain power outside coercive violence; as the guarantee repeated daily that this threat is averted. The leader's word conceals within it the ambiguity of being diverted from the function of communication that is immanent to language. There is so little necessity for the chief's discourse to be listened to that the Indians often pay no attention to it. The language of authority, the Urubu say, is a *ne eng hantan*: a *harsh* language that awaits no response. But this harshness does not compensate in the slightest for the impotence of the political institution. To the externality of power corresponds the isolation of its speech, which – because it is uttered harshly so as not to be understood – bears witness to its gentleness.

Polygyny can be interpreted in the same manner: beyond its formal aspect as a pure and simple gift meant to posit power as a rupture of exchange, a positive function takes form, one analogous to that of goods and language. The chief, as custodian of the essential values of the group, is by that very fact responsible for it, and via the women he is in a sense the group's prisoner.

This mode of constituting the political sphere can be understood, therefore, as a veritable defense mechanism for Indian societies. The culture asserts the predominance of what it is based on – exchange – precisely by treating power as the negation of that foundation. But it should be pointed out that by depriving the "signs" of their exchange value in the domain of power, these cultures take from women, goods, and words their function as signs to be exchanged; and consequently, it is as pure values that these elements are grasped, for communication ceases to be their horizon. The status of language suggests with a special force this conversion from the condition of signs to that of values: the chief's discourse recalls, by its solitude, the speech of a poet for whom words are values before they are signs. What can be the meaning, then, of this twofold process of de-signification and valorization of the elements of exchange? Perhaps it expresses – even beyond the attachment of culture to its values – the hope or nostalgia for a mythical time in which everyone would accede to the fullness of a bliss unlimited by the exigency of exchange.

Indian cultures are cultures anxious to reject a power that fascinates them: the affluence of the chief is the group's daydream. And it is clearly for the purpose of expressing both the culture's concern for itself and the dream it has of transcending itself, that power, paradoxical by its nature, is venerated in its impotence: this is the Indian chief, a metaphor for the tribe, the *imago* of its myth.

Independence and Exogamy[1]

The strongly marked contrast between the cultures of the Andean high plateaus and the cultures of the Tropical Forest, etched in the narratives and reports of sixteenth- and seventeenth-century missionaries, soldiers, and explorers, was subsequently exaggerated: there gradually formed the popular imagery of a pre-Columbian America delivered over to *savagery*, except for the Andean region where the Incas had assured the triumph of *civilization*.

These simplistic notions – naive in appearance only, for they were in complete accord with the objectives of white coloniza-

1. One omission will likely cause some surprise: the absence of the numerous tribes belonging to the important Gé linguistic stock. It is certainly not my intention to take up again in these pages the classification of the HSAI *(Handbook of South American Indians)*, which assigns to these peoples the status of Marginals, when in fact their ecology, of which agriculture is a part, should assimilate them to the cultural region of the Tropical Forest. These tribes are not touched upon in this essay precisely because of the extraordinary complexity of their social organization into clans, multiple systems of moieties, associations, and so on. For this reason, the Gé require a special study. And, moreover, it is not the least of the *Handbook*'s paradoxes to have incorporated some very rudimentary socio-political models into the well-developed ecology of the Forest, while the Gé, whose sociological composition is extremely rich, are seen as stagnating at a distinctly pre-agricultural level.

tion – crystallized in a tradition whose weight was felt heavily by Americanist ethnology in its infancy. Faithful to its calling, this ethnology selected and discussed problems in scientific terms. Nevertheless, it allowed an unmistakable persistence of traditional thought patterns to show in its solutions, a *state of mind* which, unknown to the authors, partly determined their research perspectives. What indicates this state of mind? First, a certainty: primitives are generally incapable of achieving *good* sociological models; next, a method that caricatures the most conspicuous traits of the cultures studied.

The Inca empire, for example, impressed the early chroniclers in essence by its strong centralization of power and a mode of economic organization then unknown. Now, these aspects of Inca society were transformed by modern ethnology into totalitarianism in R. Karsten,[2] or into socialism in L. Baudin.[3] But a less ethnocentric scrutiny of the source material induces us to correct these all-too modern images of a society which was, in spite of everything, archaic; and in a recent work, Alfred Metraux[4] has pointed up the existence of centrifugal forces in Tahuantinsuyu which the Cuzco clans did not think of resisting.

As for the Forest peoples, they were not classed as anachronistic cultures; on the contrary, in close parallel to the tendency to expand the "Western" features of the Inca empire, the sociological structures of the Forest societies were presented as all the more primitive, more flimsy, less capable of dynamism, strictly limited to small units. This no doubt explains the tendency to stress the fragmented, "separatist"[5] appearance of the non-Andean communi-

2. R. Karsten, *La Civilisation de l'empire Inca*, Paris, Payot, 1952.

3. L. Baudin, *L'Empire socialiste des Incas*, Paris, Institut d'Ethnologie, 1928.

4. A. Metraux, *Les Incas*, Paris, Éditions du Seuil, 1961.

5. Robert H. Lowie, "Some Aspects of Political Organisation Among the American

ties, together with the inevitable correlate: a quasi-permanent state of war. Thus, the Forest as a cultural habitat is presented as an assortment of micro-societies each more or less resembling the others, but all at the same time hostile to one another. It is quite certain that if, like Baudin, one thinks of the Guarani Indian as an individual "whose mentality is that of a child,"[6] one cannot hope to find "adult" types of social organization. This sensitivity to the atomism of Indian societies is also noticeable in Koch-Grunberg and Kirchhoff – for example, in their often excessive use of the term "tribe" to denote any community, a practice that leads them to the surprising notion of tribal exogamy applied to the Tucano tribes of the Uaupes-Caqueta region.[7]

There is no question here of taking the opposite view, attempting somehow to bring the tribes of the Tropical Forest into line with the cultures of the Andes. And yet it does seem that the most common picture of the societies in question is not always accurate; and if, as Murdock writes, "The warlikeness and atomism of simple societies have been grossly exaggerated,"[8] the same is certainly true of South America. Hence we are called upon to re-examine the ethnographic material and re-evaluate the socio-political units of the Tropical Forest, with regard to both their nature and their interrelations.

The ethnographic information is largely contained in the monumental *Handbook of South American Indians*,[9] Volume III being devoted to the Forest cultures. This cultural region comprises a very large

Aborigines. Huxley Memorial Lecture, 1948," *Journal of the Royal Anthropological Institute of Great Britain and Ireland*, vol. LXXVIII, parts 1 and 2 (1948), pp. 11–24.

6. L. Baudin, *Une Théocratie socialiste: L'État jésuite du Paraguay*, Paris, Génin, 1962, p. 14.

7. *HSAI*, vol. III, p. 780.

8. See Georges Peter Murdock, *Social Structure*, New York, Macmillan, 1949, p. 85.

9. See *HSAI*, vol. III; Robert Lowie, "Introduction."

body of tribes, many of which belong to the three major linguistic stocks: Tupi, Carib, Arawak. All these peoples can be grouped in a common category: although subject to local variations, their ecology conforms to the same model. The Forest societies' mode of subsistence is basically agricultural, involving an agriculture limited to gardening to be sure, but one whose product in almost every case is at least as substantial as that of hunting, fishing, and gathering. Futhermore, the plants cultivated are fairly constantly the same, with similar production techniques and work routines. Hence, in this instance, the ecology furnishes a very valuable basis for classification, and one is confronted with a group of societies offering, from this standpoint, a real homogeneity. It is not surprising, therefore, to find that the uniformity at the level of the "infrastructure" is ascribed to the level of the "superstructures" as well – the level, that is, of the types of social and political organization. Thus, the most widespread sociological model in the area under consideration seems to be, if we are to believe the general documentation, that of the "extended family." This is the unit moreover, that constitutes the politically autonomous community, sheltered by the great communal house or *maloca*; it holds true for the tribes inhabiting the Guianas – those of the Jurua-Purus region, the Witoto, the Peba, the Jivaro, the numerous Tupi tribes, and so on. The demographic size of these households may vary from 40-odd to several hundred persons, although the optimal mean appears to be situated between one and two hundred persons per *maloca*. There are notable exceptions to the rule: the large Apiaca, Guarani, and Tupinamba villages, which brought together up to a thousand individuals.

But this raises a twofold series of problems. The first difficulty has to do with the *nature* of the socio-political units of the Tropical Forest. Their sociological characterization as communities constituted by an extended family does not tally with their mean demographic size. In fact, Lowie holds to Kirchhoff's definition of this type of social organization:[10] it refers to a group consisting of a man, his wife – or wives if he is polygynous, his sons and their wives if the postmarital residence is patrilocal, his unmarried daughters, and the children of his sons. If the rule of residence is matrilocal, a man is surrounded by his daughters and their husbands, his unmarried sons, and the children of his daughters. Both types of extended family exist in the Forest habitat, the second being less common than the first and clearly predominating only in the Guianas and the Jurua-Purus region. The difficulty comes from the fact that an extended family, defined *strictu sensu*, could not attain the usual size of the Forest communities, that is, around a hundred persons. An extended family actually includes only three generations of relatives connected in direct line; and what is more, as Kirchhoff makes clear,[11] a process of segmentation subjects the extended family to a perpetual transformation that prevents it from going beyond a certain population level. Consequently, it is not possible for the socio-political units of the Forest to be made up of a *single* extended family and at the same time to group together a hundred persons or more. It must be admitted, therefore, if the contradiction is to be eliminated, that either the figures put forward are inexact or else an error was committed in identifying the type of social organization. And as it is surely easier to be mistaken about the "dimensions" of a society than about its nature, it is the latter that needs to be examined.

The Indian community of the Forest is described, as we have seen, as a self-contained unit with political independence as one of its essential characteristics. Thus there would be throughout this immense area a multitude of settlements, each existing for itself, the relations between them very often mutually antagonistic,

10. See *Zeitschrift für Ethnologie*, vol. LXIII (1931), pp. 85–193.

11. See Herbert Kirchhoff, *Venezuela*, Buenos Aires, 1956, Chap. 4.

that is, warlike. And it is at this point that the second difficulty emerges. For, besides the fact that generally primitive societies are wrongly condemned to a fragmentation thought to reveal a "primitiveness" that would appear in the political domain alone, the ethnological status of the Indian peoples of the Tropical Forest exhibits an additional peculiarity: if these peoples are in fact grouped within a distinct cultural unit, it is to the precise extent that they are different from the other non-Andean peoples, that is the so-called marginals and submarginals.[12] The latter are culturally defined by the nearly general and complete absence of agriculture. Hence, they consist of nomadic groups of hunters, fishermen, and gatherers: Fuegians, Patagonians, Guayaki, and the like. It is evident that these peoples can exist only in small groups scattered over vast territories. But this vital need to scatter no longer plagues the Forest people since, as sedentary growers, they are able, so it seems, to bring into play sociological models very different from those of their less favored marginal neighbors. Is it not strange to see a nomadic type of social organization and an ecology of food growers coexist in one and the same general group, especially as the growers' capabilities for transport and travel by river navigation would allow them to intensify "external" relations? Is it really possible for the benefits – enormous in some respects – of agriculture and sedentary life to vanish in such a manner? That ecologically marginal peoples might be capable of inventing highly refined sociological models offers no impossibility: the Bororo of central Brazil, with their clan organization cut across by a double system of moieties, or the Guaycuru of the Chaco, with their hierarchy of castes, are cases in point. But the converse, whereby agricultural peoples would be organized according to marginal schemes, is harder to imagine. Hence the

12. *HSAI*, vol. V, pp. 669ff.

question arises of knowing whether the political isolation of each community is a feature that is relevant to the ethnology of the Tropical Forest.

But what is wanted first is to explain the nature of these communties. That this nature is in fact problematical seems to be clearly indicated by the terminological ambiguity found repeatedly throughout the *Handbook*. If, in Volume III, Lowie calls the most prevalent socio-political unit of the area an "extended family," Stewart, in Volume V, calls it a "lineage," thus suggesting the inadequacy of the term proposed by Lowie. But while the units in question are too "populous" to be made up of a single extended family, it does not appear that we are in the presence of lineages in the strict sense either, i.e., groups with unilineal descent. In South America, and particularly in the Tropical Forest area, bilateral descent actually seems to predominate. The possession of more varied and complete genealogies would perhaps enable us to ascertain whether it is a matter of several instances of unilineal organization. But the material currently available does not permit us to assign this latter type of organization to any but a small number of Forest societies: peoples of the Para region (the Mundurucu and the Maué) or of the Uaupes-Caqueta (the Cubeo, the Tucano, and so forth).

Nor, obviously, is it a matter of kindreds: the postmarital residence, which is never neolocal, serves to determine the composition of the units, from the mere fact that with each generation, and supposing that the sex ratio is statistically in equilibrium, one half of the siblings (either the brothers where residence is matrilocal, or the sisters where it is patrilocal) leave the community of origin and go to live in the spouse's community. In a sense then, the rules of marriage assign the group an effective unilineality, even if it is not culturally recognized by the group's members, since the latter happen to be consanguineous relatives in matrilineal or patrilineal descent, depending on the rule of residence adopted. No doubt that is what decided Stewart to identify the sociological units of the Forest as lineages. It is appropriate, however, to note that if the notion of the extended family falls short, failing to account for a large part of the concrete reality of these groups, the notion of lineage, for its part, imputes to them a certain number of features they obviously do not possess. For a true lineage implies a descent that is articulated according to a unilineal mode, while here it is bilateral in the majority of cases; and, most important, the fact of belonging to the unilineal type of grouping is independent of the place of residence. Hence, in order for the communities of the Tropical Forest to be the equivalent of lineages, all their members, *including* those whom marriage has removed from the *maloca* in which they were born, would have to continue to be a part of the respective communities, on the same footing with the others. That is, the postmarital residence would not change their social status.

Now the units in question are primarily residential, and a change of residence indeed seems to entail a change of membership, or at least a break in the status held prior to marriage. What is involved here is a classic problem of ethnology: that of the relationship between a rule of residence and a mode of descent. In point of fact, it is evident that a patrilocal rule of residence, for example, is of a sort to strongly favor the establishment of a patrilineal mode of descent, which is to say, a lineal structure with a harmonic regime. But no ineluctable mechanism is at work in this, there is no categorical imperative to go from the rule of residence to that of filiation; there is simply a possibility depending largely on the concrete historical circumstances, a strong possibility to be sure, but still insufficient to allow for a close identification of the groups, since the determination of membership cannot be made "free" of the rule of residence.

If, therefore, it cannot be a matter of true lineages, that must not be allowed to mask the very real activity – one that perhaps has not received enough attention – of a twofold dynamic process which, although permanently interrupted by the Conquest, appears to have been gradually transforming the Tropical Forest communities precisely into lineages. The first component of this process, which will be discussed below, concerns the mutual relations of the different units; the second operates within each unit taken separately and relates to the unilocality of residence. Again, it should be remarked that what is involved is really only a single process – but with a double impetus, external and internal, whose effects (far from cancelling one another) amplify and reinforce one another, as I shall try to show.

Is it possible, after this survey of the reasons that prevent us from regarding the units of the Tropical Forest as extended families or as lineages, to assign them a positive denomination? Now that we know what they are not and are familiar with some of their basic distinguishing features, the difficulty comes down finally to a simple question of terminology: what are we to call these communities? They comprise from one to two hundred persons on the average; their system of descent is generally bilateral; they practice local exogamy, and the postmarital residence is either patrilocal or matrilocal, so that a certain "rate" of unilineality is evidenced. Hence, we are dealing in this instance with veritable *exogamic demes*, in Murdock's sense of the term,[13] that is, with primarily residential units, but where the exogamy and the unilocality of residence contradict, to a certain extent, the bilaterality of descent, giving these units the appearance of lineages or even clans.

What about the composition of these demes then? If the commu-

13. See Murdock, *Social Structure*.

nities, instead of being demes, amounted to extended families as Kirchhoff and Lowie suggest, the question would be somewhat academic. But, as we have seen, the demographic facts make this hypothesis untenable. Yet that does not mean this model of social organization does not exist in the Tropical Forest: it simply ceases to have the same bounds as the local community itself, which extends well beyond it. The model holds firm in the cultures of the Forest, but loses its qualification as a maximum, so to speak, in order to become the *minimum* component of social organization: that is, each deme consists of a *plurality* of extended families; and these, far from being unrelated to one another and merely juxtaposed within the same grouping, are, on the contrary, connected in a patri- or matrilineal descent line. Furthermore, this makes it possible to infer that, contrary to what Kirchhoff has written, the genealogical depth of these units exceeds three generations, even if the Indians have no precise recollection of these ties. Thus we again encounter the previously disclosed tendency to unilineality.

In this regard it is reasonable to think that the most common type of dwelling in the area, the great communal house or *maloca*, expresses this basic dimension on the plane of spatial distribution. As for the question of the number of extended families that constitute a deme, it obviously depends on the size of the units: we could nevertheless estimate it at three or four for the smallest groups (40 to 60 persons: an Aiari River community included 40 persons), and at 10 or 12 for the largest (100 to 200 persons: a Mangeroma community in the Jurua-Purus numbered 258 persons), supposing that each extended family brings together between 15 and 20 persons.

To speak of these demes as socio-political units implies that they function within the unitary scheme of "organic" totalities, and that the integration of the component elements is profound:

something conveyed by the existence of an "ésprit de corps" acting as the group's self-consciousness, and by a permanent solidarity of its members. In this sense K. Oberg is correct in seeing these collectivities as "homogeneous societies", that is, with no social stratification or horizontal segmentation.[14] The cleavages that affect them are those of sex, age, and kinship lines: and the coalescence just alluded to is expressed in the nearly always collective character of the activities essential to the life of the group: building the house, clearing garden plots, the work of harvesting, religious life, and so forth.

Is this homogeneity met with again as an integral feature at all levels of social existence? An affirmative reply would lead to the idea that archaic societies are, ipso facto, simple societies, and that differences or conflict are absent from their sociology. Now this possibility seems established at least in one domain: that of political authority. But we know, on the one hand, that each community is administered by a chief; and, on the other, that each element of the structure, each extended family that is, also has its leader, the eldest man as a rule. In appearance this poses no problem: for reasons explained elsewhere there is no "race for power" in these societies; furthermore, the inheritance of the political office seems to lay all questions to rest. Yet the fact remains that, far from being indivisible, as it were, authority does divide and becomes multiple; that by retaining its own leader each extended family thereby expresses its "will" to maintain – in a way that may or may not be emphatic – its identity. This releases forces within the group that may be divergent. Of course, this trend does not go so far as to threaten to disintegrate the group, and it is precisely at this juncture that the chief's major function intervenes: his job as

14. Kalervo Oberg, "Types of Social Structure Among the Lowland Tribes of South and Central America," *American Anthropologist*, vol. LVII, no. 3 (June 1955), pp. 472–87.

peacemaker, as an "integrator" of differences. Thus the social structure of the group and the structure of its power are seen to ratify, attract, and complete one another, each finding in the other the meaning of its own necessity and its own justification: it is because there is a central institution, a principal leader expressing the real existence of the community – and this existence is experienced as a unification – that the community can permit itself, as it were, a certain quantum of centrifugal force that is actualized in each group's tendency to preserve its individuality.

Conversely, the multiplicity of divergent trends legitimates the unifying activity of the main chieftainship. The equilibrium within the dualism of the peripheral and focal, a product of constant effort, should not be confused with the simple homogeneity of a whole, more appropriate to a geometrical arrangement of parts than the inventiveness immanent to culture. For ethnological inquiry this means analyzing the structural relationships between the various subgroups, between the subgroups and the chieftainship, with all the intrigues, tensions, resistances (apparent or not), and understandings (lasting or not) implicit in the concrete development of a society.

Thus, we see disclosed the latent and somewhat furtive presence of *differences* and their ultimate potential for open conflict; a presence that is not external to the nature of the group but, on the contrary, is a dimension of collective life engendered by the social structure itself. This takes us far from the neat simplicity of archaic societies. A careful and prolonged observation of primitive societies would show that they are no more immediately transparent than our own; and a study like that conducted by Buell Quain of the Trumai of the upper Xingu helps give the lie to this ethnocentric preconception.[15] Primitive societies, like Western

15. See R. Murphy and B. Quain, *The Trumai Indians of Central Brazil*, New York, J.-J. Augustin, 1955.

societies, are perfectly capable of handling the possibility of difference within identity, of otherness in homogeneity; and in their rejection of the mechanistic can be read the sign of their creativity.

Such, then, appears to be the shape – perhaps more faithful to the reality – of these Indian societies strung along the entire immensity of the Amazon basin: they are exogamic demes made up of a few extended families joined by matrilineal or patrilineal descent. And although they exist and function as genuine units, they nonetheless allow their elements a certain "play." But ethnographic tradition has placed heavy emphasis on the self-sufficiency, the political independence of these communities, on the separatism of Indian cultures. Had we accepted it we would be dealing with small societies living as though in a closed vessel, relatively hostile to one another, and establishing their mutual relations in the framework of a very developed model of war. This view of their "foreign relations," if it can be put that way, is closely bound up with the image of their nature first proposed. And as an examination of the latter led us to conclusions that were appreciably different, an analysis of their "being-together" is called for: that is what we will turn to now.

One fact must be acknowledged immediately: the great majority of these peoples practice local exogamy.

It is difficult, no doubt, to establish absolutely, that is, on the basis of proven facts, the generality of this institution. For while the technology and even the mythology of numerous South American tribes are often well known to us, unfortunately, the same thing cannot be said about their sociology. And yet, however sketchy and sometimes contradictory the usable information may be as to the near-universality of local exogamy, certain data make possible at least extreme probability, if not absolute certainty. Generally speaking, the number of peoples about whom we possess valid information is very small compared to the total number of ethnic groups accounted for. By making use of the material collected in the *Handbook* (Volume III) and in the *Outline of South American Cultures* by G. Murdock, we can estimate the number of ethnic groups belonging to the Tropical Forest area at approximately 130. But precise facts regarding the status of marriage are only given for 32 tribes, or around one-fourth of the total. Now, of these 32 tribes, 26 are presented as practicing local exogamy, while the remaining 6 are composed of endogamous communities.

This means that local exogamy is present in three-fourths of the tribes for which we possess concrete data. Hence, there remain a hundred tribes whose marriage rules are unknown to us, at least from this standpoint. But it can be assumed that the proportion of exogamous and endogamous tribes occurring among the known tribes stays about the same for the unknown tribes: that leads us to accept, not as a certainty (the latter is forever beyond our grasp since a large part of the Indian tribes has disappeared), but as a partly verified hypothesis, the idea that at least three-fourths of the peoples of the Tropical Forest practice local exogamy. It should be mentioned, in addition, that some ethnic groups clearly identified as endogamous (for example, the Siriono, the Bacairi, and the Tapirapé) are groups that are small in number or isolated in the midst of culturally different peoples. And lastly, it is appropriate to remark that the tribes in which local exogamy is confirmed belong to the principal linguistic families of the Forest (Arawak, Carib, Tupi, Chibcha, Pano, Peba, etc.), and that, far from being localized, they are spread across the entire area, from eastern Peru (the Amahuaca and Yagua tribes), the Guianas (the Yecuana tribes), and Bolivia (the Tacana tribes).

If our statistical scrutiny of the tribes of the Tropical Forest proves the likelihood of the vast compass of local exogamy, the latter in a great number of cases is even present of necessity, given the nature of the community. Should a single *maloca* house the entire group, the members composing it mutually acknowledge one another as real consanguineous kin when the group is made up of one or two extended families, and as fictitious or classificatory consanguines when the group is more substantial. In all cases, the people living together in the same *maloca* are closely related among themselves; hence, we can expect to find a prohibition of marriage within the group, that is, the prescription of local exogamy. Its presence is not due merely to one of its functions which, as we shall see later, is to obtain political advantages: it is owing first of all to the nature of the communities that practice it, communities whose main characteristic is that they group together only relatives classed as siblings. This excludes the possibility of Ego marrying inside the group. In a word, the community's residence in one great house and its culturally recognized membership in the same group of relatives establish the groups of the Tropical Forest as sociological units between which exchanges take place and alliances are arranged: exogamy, which is both precondition and means, is essential to the structure of these units and to their preservation as such. And, in fact, the local character of this exogamy is merely contingent, since it is a consequence of the geographic distance separating the communities. When the latter move closer to each other and exist side by side to form a village, as happens among the Tupi peoples, exogamy does not disappear though it ceases to be local. It changes into lineage exogamy.

From the outset, then, an opening is established to the outside, to the other communities. Now, this opening jeopardizes the too frequently asserted principle of absolute autonomy for each unit. It would be surprising if groups engaged in the exchange of women (where residence is patrilocal) or of sons-in-law (where it is matrilocal) – that is, involved in a *positive* relation vital to the existence of every group as such – were to simultaneously challenge the positive nature of this link by asserting extreme independence.

This independence – questionable because so much importance has been attached to it – would have a negative value since it implies a mutual hostility that can quickly develop into war. Of course there is no question of denying that these communities lead a completely autonomous existence in some basic respects: economic and religious life, internal political organization. But besides the fact that this autonomy remains partial, the generalized presence of local exogamy makes the total independence of each community impossible.

The exchange of women from *maloca* to *maloca*, by establishing close kinship ties between extended families and demes institutes political relations. These are not always explicit and codified, but they prevent neighboring groups allied through marriage from regarding one another as outright foreigners or indeed as avowed enemies. Hence, as an alliance of families, and beyond that, of demes, marriage contributes towards incorporating communities into a whole, certainly one that is very diffuse and fluid, but still defined by an implicit system of mutual rights and obligations; by a solidarity that is revealed when required by grave situations. The community has the assurance that in the event of food shortage or armed attack, for instance, it is surrounded by allies and relatives, not hostile strangers. The widening of the political horizon to include more than a single community does not depend solely on the contingent existence of friendly groups living nearby: it refers to each group's pressing need to provide for its security by forming alliances.

Another factor works towards establishing this sort of multicommunity structure. It is true that local exogamy effects a classing of possible spouses such that the only accessible sexual partners belong to units different from that of Ego. But the combined number of these partners is in fact limited, since only a minority of them fall in the category of preferential spouses: in reality, the rule of *cross-cousin marriage* appears to overlay that of local exogamy. So that male Ego's probable or preferable wife will be not only a woman residing in a *maloca* other than his own, but also the daughter of his mother's brother or of his father's sister. This means the exchange of women does not come about between units that are initially "indifferent" to one another, but rather between groups woven into a network of close kinship ties, even if, as is very likely the case, this kinship is more classificatory than real. Hence the kinship relationships already established and local exogamy combine their effects in order to draw each unit out of its singularity, by elaborating a *system* that transcends each of its elements.

One may wonder, however, what deep intention is behind the practice of local exogamy; if it is simply a matter of sanctioning the incest taboo by preventing marriage between co-residents, that is, between relatives, the means may seem disproportionate to the ends. Since each *maloca* houses at least one hundred persons on the average, all relatives in theory, the bilateral nature of descent precludes the comprehensive and precise recollection of genealogical connections which alone would permit an exact determination of degrees of kinship, something possible only when descent is unilineal. A man belonging to extended family "A" could marry a woman of the same *maloca* as he but belonging to extended family "B" and still not run the express risk of committing the absolute transgression, since it might very well be impossible to prove the existence of a non-fictitious kinship tie between man "A" and woman "B." Thus the function of local exogamy is not negative, to strengthen the incest taboo; but positive, to compel residents to contract marriage outside the community of origin. Or, in other words, the meaning of local exogamy lies in its function: *it is the means for entering into political alliances.*

Is it possible to estimate the number of communities that may form such a network of alliances? The almost complete lack of documents on this point appears to bar attempts at a reply, even a rough estimate. And yet, perhaps, certain data will allow us to arrive at a probable figure, or rather place it somewhere between a minimum and a maximum.

If local exogamy were permanently established only between two communities, we would be dealing with a true system of complementary exogamic moieties. But as this type of social organization, practically universal among the Gé tribes, was implemented only very rarely by the peoples of the Tropical Forest, with the exception of the Mundurucu and the Tucano, it is very probable that matrimonial exchanges took place between three communities at least. It seems, therefore, that we can take this figure as a minimum. If we further accept the idea that the specific socio-political – and ecological, too, no doubt – models of the Tropical Forest cultures achieved their most exemplary development among certain peoples belonging to the Tupi group, we can reasonably suppose that these latter reached the maximum political spread we are looking for. Now Tupinamba and Guarani villages are known to have consisted of from four to eight large collective houses. These were genuine villages, which is to say, groups concentrated in a limited territory, while the other peoples of the area lived in communities that were sometimes very far apart. We can take the greater or lesser proximity of the *maloca* as indicating a difference at the level of social and political organization.

It seems possible, therefore, to describe the distinguishing features of this area's most noteworthy type of social organization. Bearing in mind the nature of the units as discussed above, we will call these mega-units of three to eight local communities *polydemic structures*, the Tupi having furnished the best illustration of these. Thus, instead of the traditional, "tachist" picture of myriads of groups both fearful of and hostile to one another, we see the slow labor of unifying forces invalidating the hypothetical atomism of these cultures. This is accomplished by grouping them into collectivities whose size varies; but in any case, these groupings dissolve the facile image of societies whose egocentrism and aggressiveness would attest to a state of infancy.

Thus far these cultures have been viewed from the standpoint of *structure* only, that is, without any reference to a possible diachronic dimension. However, it has become evident during our study of the nature of the communities that while they are not lineages, that is, strictly unilineal organizations but rather exogamic demes, several factors can contribute to the gradual transformation of these bilateral demes into unilineal descent groups. These factors are of two kinds: some are immanent to the very structure of the deme, others act at the level of interdemic political relations. But all have a part in initiating not a history in the strict sense, certainly, but rather a *dynamic* whose motion is adapted to the extremely slow rhythms of life in these societies.

As we have seen above, co-residence creates the privileged tie between inhabitants of the same *maloca* that makes them relatives. Furthermore, the postmarital residence being defined as either patri-or matrilocal, the inevitable effect is to strongly reinforce relations of affection and solidarity between relatives descending patri- or matrilineally. In the case of patrilocal residence, for example, Ego, born in the same house as his father and his paternal grandfather, will himself spend his whole life there in the company of his patrilineal kin, that is, his grandfather's brothers and their male descendents.

The permanent structural element which serves as the framework of the deme, and around which collective life is organized, consists of a patrilineal descent group and it alone, since Ego's matrilateral kin will remain, if not entirely unknown to him, at least much more removed. As a matter of fact, male Ego's mother comes from a community which, even though linked to that of his father by kinship, will always be a rather alien group for Ego, one he will come into contact with only on rare occasions. The tie between Ego and his matrilateral kin will greatly depend on the distance that separates the houses of their parents. If it takes a walk of several days or even several hours to get from one to the other, contact with the mother's descent group will be no more than intermittent. Now the *maloca* are ordinarily constructed at considerable distances from each other, and hence it is almost exclusively to the group of patrilineal relatives that Ego will feel he belongs.

In addition, these demes also contribute an important factor to the determination of lineage: continuity. For, contrary to what Kirchhoff has stated,[16] the community – for him an extended family – is not dissolved upon the death of its chief, for the simple reason that the chieftainship is nearly always hereditary, a fact noted by Kirchhoff himself, curiously enough. The hereditary nature of the political office is a sufficient sign of the temporal endurance of the social structure. Actually, what sometimes occurs – as for example with the Witoto – is not the dispersal of the group but rather the abandonment of the house "owned" by the chief and the construction of a *maloca* in the immediate vicinity of the first house. The transmission of leadership from father to son – that is, its continuation in the patrilineal descent group that constitutes the heart of the social structure – expresses precisely the will of the group to maintain its spatio-temporal unity. The Tupinamba carried their respect for patrilineality to an extreme, since a child born to a mother belonging to the group but to a father from outside – often a prisoner of war – was swiftly devoured, while the children of a man belonging to the group were affiliated with their father's lineage. These various factors, operating at the level

16. See note 10.

of the internal organization of the deme, manifest a distinct tendency to emphasize one of the two kinship lines and ensure its continuity; the deme moves in the direction of lineage, and the motor, so to speak, of this dynamics is the contradiction between a bilateral system of descent and a unilocal residence, between bilateral legality and the unilineal reality.

We know that unilocality of residence does not necessarily lead to unilineality of descent, even if it is a necessary condition for the latter, as Murdock has shown, differing with Lowie on this point. One can speak of true lineages only if affiliation is independent of residence. The patrilocal demes of the Tropical Forest would be lineages if the women continued to be a part of their group of origin, even after their departure due to marriage. But as it happens, the distance between the great houses, which assures that the woman leaves virtually for good, prevents this tendency to organize into lineages from developing further, because for a woman marriage is tantamount to disappearing. Hence it is possible to say that in all the sectors of the Tropical Forest in which, by virtue of the wide separation of the *maloca*, the polydemic structures are fluid, the tendency to lineages cannot materialize.

The same is not true where this type of structure is more clear-cut, more pronounced, more crystallized: the big Guarani and Tupinamba villages. In them, spatial contiguity eliminates the movement of persons: all the young man does during the years of "service" owed to his father-in-law, or the young woman when she marries, is to change *maloca*. Hence every individual remains under the continual gaze of his or her family and in daily contact with their descent group of origin. Among these peoples, therefore, nothing stands in the way of the conversion of demes into lineages, especially in view of the other forces that come to support this trend. For if the Tupi carried to completion models that are merely sketched out by the other Forest peoples, that is, effecting a thorough integration of the socio-political units into a structured whole, it is because there were centripetal currents whose presence is attested by the concentrated village structure. But it then must be asked, what becomes of the units within this new organization? Two possibilities are open here: either the tendency to unification and integration is manifested in the gradual dissolution of these elemental units – or at least a substantial reduction of their structural functions – and the resulting appearance of the initial stages of social stratification; or else the units hold their ground and gain in strength.

The first possibility was realized by the peoples of northwestern South America (the Chibcha and the Arawak of the islands, for example), consolidated under the heading of the Circum-Caribbean cultural area.[17] These regions, Colombia and northern Venezuela in particular, witnessed the creation of a good many little "states," fiefdoms often limited to one town or valley. There, aristocracies in control of the religious and military power ruled over a mass of "plebians" and a large class of slaves taken in war against neighboring peoples. The second possibility appears to have been embraced by the Tupi, since no social stratification existed among them. As a matter of fact, it is not possible to put Tupinamba prisoners of war in the same category as a social class of slaves whose labor power was appropriated by their masters and conquerors. The first chroniclers of Brazil, for example, Thevet,[18] Léry,[19] or Staden,[20] relate that the possession, of one or more prisoners of war generated so much social prestige for the Tupinamba warriors

17. See *HSAI*, vols. IV and V.

18. A. Thevet *Le Brésil et les Brésiliens*, Paris, P.U.F., 1953, p. 93.

19. Jean de Léry, *Journal de bord ... en la terre de Brésil, 1557*, Paris, Éditions de Paris, 1952.

20. Hans Staden, *Véritable histoire et description d'un pays ... situé dans le Nouveau Monde nommé Amerique*, Paris, A. Bertrand, 1837.

that whenever food was scarce, the latter preferred to go without eating rather than deprive their captives of nourishment. Moreover, the prisoners were very soon assimilated into their masters' community, and the captor had no qualms about giving his sister or daughter in marriage to this living proof of his valor. And the incorporation proved complete when, after a period of time that was often quite long, the killing of the prisoner transformed him into ceremonial food for his masters.

Thus Tupi societies were not stratified; consequently, the divisions and lines of force they were built around were the same as in the rest of the area: sex, age, kinship, and so forth. And what is more, the tightening and contraction of the general model of multicommunity social organization, with the village as its spatial expression, did not operate as a unifying principle calling into question the "personality" of each of its elements, in this instance demes; on the contrary, the very emergence of such a centripetal force aiming at the crystallization of a "floating" structure caused a symmetrical strengthening of the centrifugal forces immanent to the structure of demes. In other words, the dynamic described here is *dialectical* in nature; for, as the construction of the system progressively asserts and defines itself, its component elements react to this change in their status by accentuating their concrete and special nature, their individuality. So that the advent of the global structure produces not a suppression of the demes – an event that would make possible another kind of differentiation, namely social stratification – but a structural modification of the units.

What direction will this transformation take? The answer rests completely with determinations that are characteristic of the units themselves: they are basically kinship groups. Then what means will the latter have to remold themselves in terms of a development that renders them identical by unifying them? They will bring to the fore the latent unilineality that is their distinctive attribute, and will center the law of membership not on a co-residency that ceases to be of primary importance, but on the rule of filiation: hence the demes change into lineages, and the transformation of the elements becomes bound up with the constitution of the global structure. The Tupi peoples thus furnish us with an illustration of the *transition from a polydemic structure to a multilineage structure.*

Does this mean that the lineages appear only as a reaction to a new organization of a group of residential units and in relation to it? It is obviously not possible to maintain this, because residence and filiation do not follow from one another. The transition in itself is contingent, that is, it is linked to history and not to structure: as for the Tupi, the catalytic agency, in what was present only potentially and as a tendency among the other peoples of the Tropical Forest, was the anxiety that impelled them to erect more "constricted" social structures. Different historical processes might very well bring about this transition. But it can be stressed that the mutation of a deme into a lineage stimulates the inherent *relational* qualities of each unit. There are no lineages except in a "strong" system. Conversely, the rise of such a system culminates either in a social stratification that negates the structuring value of the rules of filiation, or else in the confirmation and even overvaluation of these rules: it might be said that lineage is *diacritical* in nature. It is as if the centripetal motion fostering political relations in a society previously fluid, and creating internal disequilibrium, simultaneously produced the countervailing means. Centrifugal forces – forces corresponding to the new situation – are brought into play at the elemental level, and enable the society to reach a new equilibrium. In the last analysis, the forces "working" on these primitive societies aim, directly or indirectly, at securing an equilibrium that is constantly endangered.

Moreover, it is certain that the Tupi version of the sociological model typical of the Forest does not lend itself to the continued existence of the internal relations described at the level of the deme. The emergence of the lineage structure, that is, the contraction of the genealogical connections by which its unitary character is affirmed, greatly diminishes the functional value of the subgroups or extended families that constitute the lineage. That is why the relevant question in the case of the Tupi is interlineage relationships.

Each Tupi village consisted of a cluster averaging from four to eight great houses, each sheltering a lineage and having its leader. But the village as such was under the guidance of a chief. The Tupinamba community raises the question of political relations to a degree unknown in the rest of the Forest: as a multilineage structure, it provides itself with a "centralized" authority and yet preserves the "local" subchieftainships. No doubt in response to this dualism of power, a "council of elders" was formed among these Indians, a body whose approval was necessary for the exercise of authority by the main chief.

The peoples of the Tupi-Guarani group are set apart from the other ethnic groups of the same cultural area by the greater complexity of their political problematic, tied to the sometimes immense widening of their horizon. But it seems the Tupi did not restrict this expansion to establishing multilineage village communities. In many zones of the Forest the tendency developed to construct a model of authority extending well beyond the confines of a single village. We know that, generally speaking, intertribal relations were much closer and more sustained than the emphasis on the bellicose spirit of these peoples would lead us to believe. Various authors, Lévi-Strauss[21] and Métraux,[22] among others, have effectively shown that commercial exchanges between groups, some-

21. Claude Lévi-Strauss, "Guerre et commerce chez les indiens de l'Amérique du Sud," *Renaissance*, vol. I, parts 1 and 2.

22. A. Métraux, *La Civilisation matérielle des tribus Tupi-Guarani*, Paris, P. Geuthner, 1928, p. 277.

times located very far apart, were frequently intense. Now, with the Tupi, it is not solely a matter of commercial relations, but of a real territorial and political *expansion*, with some chiefs exercising authority over several villages. Let us recall the image of the famous Tama chief, Quoniambec, who made such a sharp impression on Thevet and Staden. "This King was much venerated by all the Savages, yea even by those who were not of his land, so good a warrior was he in his time, and so widely did he lead them in battle."[23] These same chroniclers inform us, moreover, that the authority of the Tupinamba chiefs was never so strong as in time of war, their power then all but absolute and the discipline imposed on their troops unanimously respected. Hence the number of warriors that a chief could muster is the best indication of the extent of his authority. To be precise, the figures cited are at times – taking everything into consideration – enormous: Thevet gives a maximum of 12,000 "Tabaiarres and Margageaz" combatting one another in a single engagement. In a similar situation, Léry gives a maximum of 10,000 men and the figure 4,000 for a skirmish he witnessed. Following his masters into combat, Staden counted, on the occasion of a sea attack against Portuguese positions, 38 boats containing 18 men on the average, or nearly 700 men for the small village of Ubatuba alone.[24] As it is appropriate to multiply the number of warriors by approximately four, in order to obtain the number of the total population, we see there were veritable federations among the Tupinamba, grouping together from 10 to 20 villages. Hence the Tupi, and in particular those inhabiting the Brazilian coast, display a very clear tendency towards establishing far-reaching political systems, with powerful chieftainships whose structure needs to be analyzed. By enlarging its boundaries, the

23. Ibid., p. 93.

24. Ibid., p. 178, note 2.

field of application of a centralized authority creates bitter conflicts with the small local centers of power. Thus the question arises of the nature of the relationships between the main chieftainship and the subchieftainships: for instance, between "King" Quoniambec and the "kinglets, his vassals."

The coastal Tupi are not alone in exhibiting such tendencies. To cite a more recent example, we call attention to the Tupi-Kawahib as well. At the beginning of the century one of their groups, the Takwatip, extended its hegemony gradually over the neighboring tribes, under the direction of its chief, Abautara, whose son Lévi-Strauss met.[25] Similar processes were observed among the Omagua and the Cocama. These were Tupi peoples occupying the middle and upper reaches of the Amazon, among whom the authority of a chief was brought to bear not only on the great house but on the community in its entirety: the size of the latter could be quite substantial, seeing that an Omagua village was said to comprise 60 houses, each one lodging from 50 to 60 persons.[26] It should be noted further that the Guarani, culturally closely related to the Tupinamba, also possessed highly developed chieftainships.

But by viewing Tupi culture in its political dynamics as founding "kingdoms," is there not the risk of laying too much stress on its originality compared with the Tropical Forest as a whole, assuming it to be a cultural entity independent of the area in which we first situated it? That would amount to disregarding identical processes, though much smaller in scale, among peoples belonging to other linguistic stocks. We are reminded, for example, that the Jivaro too presented this model of multicommunity organization, since military alliances were concluded between local groups: it

25. Claude Lévi-Strauss, *Tristes Tropiques*, John Russell, trans., New York, Criterion Books, 1961, Chap. XXXI.

26. See *HSAI*, vol. III.

is in this fashion that several *jivaria* – the *maloca* of these Indians – joined forces to wage war against the Spanish. In addition, the Carib tribes of the Orinoco used local exogamy as a means to extend political hegemony over several communities. In varying ways, then, the Forest reveals the tendency to establish social groupings that are more wide-ranging than anywhere else on the continent.

It should not be forgotten, however, that the strength of this trend varied with the concrete – economic, demographic, and religious – circumstances of the cultures in which it was manifested. The difference between the Tupi and the other societies was not in kind but in degree; this implies, consequently, that they were not only better able than the others to build on the plane of social structure a model of organization they shared. It also means the dynamics immanent to the Forest cultures acquired a faster rhythm and acceleration among the Tupi than elsewhere.

Granted, the Amerindian societies were archaic, but negatively so, if you will, and then only in relation to our European criteria. Is this reason enough to term cultures "stationary" whose development does not conform to our own schemata? Must these societies be seen as having no history? Before the question can have any meaning, it is necessary to frame it in such a way as to make a reply possible, that is, without postulating the universality of the Western model. History declares itself in manifold ways, and changes according to the different perspectives in which it is viewed: "The opposition between progressive cultures and static cultures thus seems to result, first, from a difference of focus."[27]

The tendency to form a *system*, unevenly realized in depth and extension depending on the region considered, leads us because of these very differences to grant the cultures of this area a "dia-

27. Claude Lévi-Strauss, *Structural Anthropology*, Monique Layton, trans., New York, Basic Books, 1976, vol. II, p. 340.

chronic" dimension, one that can be located notably among the Tupi-Guarani: hence, these are not societies without history. It is on the level of political organization much more than in the ecological domain that the sharpest antithesis is to be found between marginal and Forest cultures. But neither are they historical societies. In this sense the symmetrical and inverse contrast with the Andean cultures is just as strong. Therefore, the political dynamic that assigns the Forest societies their specificity would place them on a structural plane – and not at a chronological stage – that we might call *prehistorical*. The Marginals furnish the example of a-historical societies, the Incas of an already historical culture. It appears reasonable, then, to assume that the dynamics characteristic of the Tropical Forest is a *condition of possibility* for the kind of history that conquered the Andes. The political problematic of the Forest refers to the two planes that set its limits: the genetic plane of the birthplace of the institution, and the historical plane of its destiny.

Elements of Amerindian Demography

Some may be surprised that a text concerned mainly with demography should accompany studies devoted to political anthropology. There is no compelling reason, it would seem, to invoke such evidence as the size and density of the societies under scrutiny when the object is to analyze the functioning of power relations and the institutions that govern them. There is thought to exist a kind of autonomy of the sphere of power (or non-power), maintaining and reproducing itself apart from and protected from any external influences, as for example the size of the population. And, in fact, this idea of a tranquil relationship between the group and its form of power appears to correspond fairly closely to the reality presented by archaic societies, which know and practice many methods for controlling and preventing the growth of their population: abortion, infanticide, sexual taboos, late weaning, and so on. Now this ability of the savages to code the flux of their demography has gradually validated the belief that a primitive society is necessarily a "restricted" society, since we are told that the so-called subsistence economy would not be able to supply the needs of a large population.

The traditional image of South America (let us not forget this image was drawn in large part by ethnology itself) is an exceptionally good illustration of that mixture of half-truths, errors, and prejudices which results in facts being treated with astonishing light-mindedness (see, in the *Handbook of South American Indians*, the classification of South American societies).[1] On the one side, the Andes and the Highland cultures which succeeded each other in that region; on the other, all the rest: forests, savannas, and pampas, teeming with small societies, all similar, a monotonous repetition of the same that appears to display no difference. It is not so much a question of how much truth there is in all this, but rather of gauging the extent of falsehood. To return to the point of departure, the problem of the connection between demography and political authority divides into two lines of inquiry: (1) Are all the forest societies of South America on a par with one another at the level of the socio-political units of which they consist? (2) Does the nature of political power remain unchanged when its field of demographic application expands and grows more dense?

It was in discussing the chieftainship in Tupi-Guarani societies that we met the demographic problem. This group of tribes, very homogeneous both linguistically and culturally, offers two rather remarkable characteristics that mark them off clearly from the other Forest societies. First, the chieftainship asserted itself with greater force among these Indians than elsewhere; secondly, the demographic density of the social units – the local groups – was distinctly higher than the mean densities commonly accepted as normal for South American societies. While not asserting that the transformation of political power among the Tupi-Guarani was

1. For facts relating to the sixteenth, seventeenth, and eighteenth centuries, my reference sources throughout are the French, Portuguese, Spanish, German, etc., chroniclers, as well as the texts and letters of the first Jesuits in South America. These sources are sufficiently well known to make further details superfluous. In addition, I have consulted the *Handbook of South American Indians*, New York, 1963, vol. V.

caused by demographic expansion, it seems to us at least justifiable to place these two specific dimensions of these tribes in perspective. But at this point a significant question arises: were the local groups of the Tupi-Guarani actually much larger than those of other cultures?

This brings up the whole problem of sources and the credence they should be granted. The Tupi-Guarani achieve the paradox of having almost completely vanished long ago (all but a few thousand of them who survive in Paraguay) and of being nonetheless perhaps the best-known indigenous people of South America. A very abundant literature is available about them: that of the first explorers, soon followed by the Jesuits who, coming from France, Spain, and Portugal as early as the mid-sixteenth century, were able to observe at leisure these savages who occupied the entire Brazilian coast and a large part of present-day Paraguay. Thousands of pages are devoted to describing the everyday life of these Indians, their wild and cultivated plants, the way they married, raised children, and made war, their ceremonial killing of prisoners, relations between groups, etc. The firsthand accounts of these chroniclers, given at different times and places, show an ethnographic consistency that is unique in South America, where one is most often faced with an extreme linguistic and cultural fragmentation.

The Tupi-Guarani present the reverse situation: they were tribes located thousands of miles from one another, but living the same kind of life, practicing the same rites, and speaking the same language. A Guarani from Paraguay would have been on perfectly familiar ground among the Tupi of Maranhão, and yet the latter were 4,000 kilometers away. It is true, reading the old chronicles can sometimes prove tiresome, since their authors see and describe the same reality. Still, they provide a solid foundation of work since they do validate one another: Montoya and Jarque, missionaries among the Guarani of Paraguay, echo Thevet and Léry who visited the Tupinamba of Rio Bay 60 years before. So that the talent of the chroniclers, almost all of whom were learned men and faithful observers, was coupled with the relative uniformity of the peoples under observation: from their meeting, happily for Americanists, an exceptionally rich body of material is still extant, material researchers can rely on.

Nearly all the chroniclers attempted to complement their descriptions with numerical data about the dimensions of the houses, the surface area planted in crops, the distances separating the villages, and, above all, the number of inhabitants in the regions they visited. Of course, their motives varied: witness the ethnographic rigor of Léry, the military objectivity of Staden, the administrative preoccupation of the missionaries who needed to take a census of the peoples under their control. But on this point, and others too, the quantitative information, whether gathered among the Guarani or the Tupi, in Maranhão or the south of Brazil, shows no disagreement: from one end of the vast territory occupied by the Tupi-Guarani to the other, the figures recorded are much the same. Strangely enough, the specialists in South America have thus far completely ignored this data – and it is especially valuable as it is often very precise – or have rejected it outright. The reason invoked: the chroniclers grossly exaggerated the size of the native population. One is thus placed before a very unusual situation: everything the chroniclers wrote is admissable, except the figures they gave! No one seems to be bothered by the fact that the errors, if not the lies, of the chroniclers are all located within the same order of magnitude.

What needs examining first is the validity of the criticisms leveled at the chroniclers' estimates. They are for the most part collected and discussed in the work of the major specialist in Amerindian demography, Angel Rosenblatt. The method he uses to calculate the indigenous population of South America at the time of the Discovery plainly betrays the slight value he sets on the information supplied by the chroniclers. How many Indians were there in America before the coming of the white man? For a long time the answers Americanists gave to this question were as varied as they were arbitrary because they lacked a scientific basis. Thus they fluctuate, for the New World in its entirety, from 8,400,000 inhabitants in Kroeber's judgment, to 40,000,000 according to P. Rivet.

Taking up the problem of America's pre-Columbian population in his turn, Rosenblatt arrives at a figure approaching 13,000,000, of which he assigns 6,785,000 to South America. He believes that the margin of error for his estimate does not exceed 20 percent and that, therefore, his approach is rigorous and scientific. What about this rigor? He explains that "the density of the population depends ... not only on the environment but also on the economic and social structure. In studying all these peoples we have observed, as might be expected, a certain parallelism between the population density and the cultural level."[2] This qualification is vague enough to be readily accepted. What appears more debatable is the author's viewpoint when he writes:

> In particular, one finds a large population where there is established a great political formation based on agricultural modes of existence. In America, this was the case of the Aztec, Maya, Chibcha, and Inca civilizations. With them, pre-Columbian agriculture reached its zenith and dense hubs of population took shape in its midst.[3]

2. A. Rosenblatt, *La Poblacíon indígena y el mestizaje en America*, Buenos Aires, 1954, vol. I, p. 103.

3. Ibid., p. 103.

I see in this statement something like a conjuring trick: Rosenblatt is, in fact, not content to tie high population density to a technology of intensive agriculture; when he speaks of a "great political formation" he brings in, on the sly, the idea of a state. Yet, despite all it implies, this reference to the state as the mark and bearer of civilization relates only at a distance to what interests us here. The essential point comes next: "But while the great cultures reached the agricultural stage, and in Peru the llama and alpaca were successfully domesticated, *the greater part of the continent lived from hunting, fishing, and gathering*. Hunting peoples need vast prairies . . . , peoples who feed themselves from hunting and fishing are forced to practice a certain nomadism. The forest has never sheltered large populations because of the high mortality rates, difficult climatological conditions, the struggle with insects and wild beasts, the scarcity of edible plants. . . . Except for the agricultural zone, which stretched out in a narrow strip the length of the Andes . . . , *the continent in 1492 was an immense forest or steppe*."[4] It would be a mistake to believe it a waste of time to examine such a statement of nonsense, for Rosenblatt's entire demography is based on it, and his work is still the reference and the source for Americanists interested in the problem of population.

The author's approach to the subject is summary. Hunting peoples, needing a great deal of space, have a low-density population; now South America was almost entirely occupied by tribes of hunters; the native population of the continent was, therefore, very low. The implication: consequently, the estimates of the chroniclers, for example, are to be completely discounted since they put forward relatively high population figures.

It goes without saying (but it's much better said) that all this is patently false. Rosenblatt pulls from thin air an America of nomad

4. Ibid., pp. 104–05; the emphasis is mine.

hunters so as to cause acceptance of a low demographic estimate. (Although it should be noted that he shows himself to be more generous than Kroeber.) What were things like in America in 1500, then? Exactly the opposite of what Rosenblatt asserts. Most of the continent was settled by sedentary agriculturalists who were cultivating a wide variety of plants, the list of which we will not reproduce here. We can even derive an axiom from this basic fact by stating that *wherever agriculture was ecologically and technologically feasible, it was present.* Now this determination of the possible arable space takes in the immense Orinoco-Amazon-Parana-Paraguay system and even the Chaco: the only region to be excluded from this habitat is the pampas that extend from Tierra del Fuego to about the 32nd parallel, a hunting and gathering territory occupied by the Tehuelche and Puelche tribes. Hence, only a small part of the continent supports Rosenblatt's argument. Perhaps it will be objected that inside the zone where agriculture is feasible some peoples do not practice it. First of all, I will point out that these instances are extremely rare and localized; the Guayaki of Paraguay, the Siriono of Bolivia, and the Guahibo of Colombia. Secondly, I will recall that it has been possible to verify that these are not instances of truly archaic peoples but, on the contrary, *societies that have lost agriculture.* For my part, I have shown that the Guayaki, who are pure hunters and nomads of the forest, gave up cultivating corn towards the end of the sixteenth century. In short, there is nothing left to support Rosenblatt's endeavor. This does not necessarily cast doubt on the figure of 6,785,000 inhabitants given by him for South America. It is simply that, like all the previous estimates, it is purely arbitrary, and it would be a matter of chance if it proved to be correct. Finally, seeing that the reason Rosenblatt gives for rejecting the precise details cited by the chroniclers turns out to be totally whimsical, we are within our rights in saying: since no valid argument nullifies the demographic data of the chroniclers – who *were eyewitnesses* – perhaps it is better, setting aside the usual prejudices, to take seriously for once what they tell us. That is what we shall try to do.

For us there is no question of taking the classic road by reckoning the Indian population of the whole of South America in 1500, an impossible task in our view. But we can attempt to determine how many Guarani Indians there were at the time. The attempt is justified for two reasons: the first relates to the disposition of their territory, which was quite homogeneous, with known and hence measurable boundaries. The same is not true of the Tupi: they inhabited almost the entire Brazilian coastland, but it is not known how far their tribes extended back into the interior; consequently, it is not possible to judge the extent of their territory. The second reason has to do with the numerical data. As will be seen, it is more plentiful than one might suppose, and of two different categories: the data obtained in the sixteenth century and the beginning of the seventeenth and that belonging to the end of the seventeenth century and the beginning of the eighteenth. The latter, supplied by the Jesuits, is concerned only with the Guarani. As for the former, it furnishes facts about the Guarani and the Tupi, but more about the Tupi than the Guarani. But these societies were so homogeneous in all respects that the demographic dimensions of the Guarani and Tupi local groups must have been very similar. It follows that while the Tupi population figures cannot be mechanically applied to the Guarani reality, at least they can be assumed to be of the same order of magnitude when there is a lack of information regarding the Guarani.

Contacts were established very early between the Indians of Brazil and the Europeans, probably in the first decade of the sixteenth century, via the French and Portuguese seafaring traders who came to exchange metal tools and cheaply made goods for brazilwood (i.e., *bois de braise*). The first letters of the Jesuit missionaries who settled among the Tupinamba date from 1549. The penetration of whites into the heart of the continent took place during the first half of the century. The Spanish, setting out in search of the Inca Eldorado, sailed up the Rio de la Plata, then the Paraguay. The first founding of Buenos Aires occurred in 1536. Under pressure from the tribes, the Conquistadors had to abandon it almost immediately and went on to found Asunción in 1537; this town later becoming the capital of Paraguay. It was then no more than a base camp for organizing expeditions of conquest and exploration directed towards the Andes from which the Spaniards were separated by the vastness of the Chaco. It was the Guarani Indians, masters of the whole region, with whom the Spanish allied themselves. These brief historical particulars explain why the Tupi-Guarani became known almost as early as the Aztecs and Incas.

What was the composition of the local groups, or villages, of the Tupi-Guarani? All the facts are well known, but there may be some point in recalling the essentials. A Guarani or Tupi village comprised four to eight large communal houses, the *maloca*, positioned around a central plaza reserved for religious and ceremonial functions. The dimensions of the *maloca* varied depending on the observers and, no doubt, on the groups visited. Their length is placed somewhere between 125 feet for the smallest and 500 feet for the largest. As to the number of occupants of each *maloca*, it fluctuated from 100 (according to Cardim, for instance) to five or six hundred (Léry). The result is that the population of the simplest Tupinamba villages (four *maloca*) must have included around 400 persons, whereas that of the most substantial (seven or eight *maloca*) reached, or exceeded, three thousand persons. Thevet, for his part, talks about some villages where he stayed having six thousand and even ten thousand inhabitants. Let us suppose that these last figures are exaggerated. The fact remains that the demographic scale of the Tupi groups goes far beyond the ordinary size of

South American societies. By way of comparison, I will recall that among the Yanomami of Venezuela, a forest people, and moreover one that is still intact due to continued protection from contact with whites, the most populous local groups number 250 persons.

The information supplied by the chroniclers shows unmistakably that the Tupi-Guarani villages varied in size. But we can assume a mean population of 600 to a thousand persons per group, a hypothesis, it should be underscored, that is deliberately *low*. This estimate may appear enormous to Americanists. It finds confirmation not only in the impressionistic notations of the first voyagers – the multitude of children swarming in the villages – but above all in the numerical data they furnish. This information is often concerned with the military activities of the Tupinamba. As a matter of fact, the chroniclers were unanimously struck, at times horrified, by these Indians' fanatical taste for warfare. The French and the Portuguese, in armed competition over who would gain domination of the Brazilian coastland, were able to exploit this Indian bellicosity by becoming allies with tribes which were enemies of one another. Staden, for example, or Anchieta, speak as eyewitnesses of Tupinamba battle fleets comprising as many as 200 pirogues, each one carrying from 20 to 30 men. Martial expeditions sometimes involved no more than a few hundred combatants. But some, which lasted several weeks or even months, mobilized up to twelve thousand warriors, not counting the women responsible for "logistics" (the transport of "war meal" for feeding the troops). Léry tells about participating in a battle on the beaches of Rio that lasted half a day: he places at five or six thousand the number of combatants *belonging to each faction*. Naturally such concentrations, even allowing for the error inherent in estimates made "at a glance," were possible only provided there was an alliance of several villages. But the relationship between the number of men old enough to fight and the total number of the population gives clear proof of the demographic amplitude of the Tupi-Guarani societies. (It ought to be understood that all questions relating to war and the number of local groups involved in the alliance networks are very relevant to both the demographic problem and the political problem. We cannot linger on these questions here. I will merely note in passing that, by their duration and the "mass formations" they brought into play, these military expeditions no longer have anything in common with what is called warfare in the other South American tribes, which nearly always consists of hit-and-run raids conducted at dawn by a handful of attackers. Beyond the difference in the nature of warfare can be glimpsed a difference in the nature of political power.)

All these facts are concerned with the Tupi of the coast. But what about the Guarani? While the Conquistadors proved to be miserly with figures regarding them, we do know that their villages, made up, as in the case of the Tupi, of four to eight *maloca*, left the first explorers with the impression of a crowd. Álvar Núñez Cabeza de Vaca, having left the Atlantic in November of 1541, reached Asunción in March of 1542. The account of this crossing of the entire Guarani territory is full of remarks concerning the number of villages visited and the number of inhabitants in each. When the Spanish, led by Domingo de Irala, arrived at the site of what is now Asunción, they made contact with the two chiefs who controlled the region: the latter could put *four thousand warriors* into the field. This is the first numerical data concerning the Guarani, the more convincing as it is precise. A short time after the conclusion of the alliance, these two caciques were able to raise what must indeed be called an army – eight thousand men who helped Irala and his soldiers combat the Agaz tribes who had risen up against the Spanish. In 1542, the latter had to give battle to a great Guarani chief, Tabaré, who commanded eight thousand warriors. In 1560, there was a new revolt of the Guarani, three thousand of whom were wiped out by their new masters. There would be no end to it, if we were to draw up a column of figures, all of which fall within the same order of magnitude. Let us cite a few more, however, from among those furnished by the Jesuits. It is known that the first "réductions," established at the beginning of the seventeenth century by Ruiz Montoya, immediately fell victim to the assaults of those who were called the *Mamelucos*. These murderous bands, made up of Portuguese and mestizos, would leave the São Paolo region in order to capture, in Guarani country, the maximum number of Indians, whom they would in turn sell as slaves to the colonists along the coast. The story of the beginning of the Missions is that of their struggle against the *Mamelucos*. In the space of a few years, the latter, so say the archives of the Jesuits, killed or took captive three hundred thousand Indians. Between 1628 and 1630, the Portuguese kidnapped sixty thousand Guarani *from the Missions*. In 1631, Montoya resigned himself to evacuating the last two remaining réductions of Guaira Province (situated, therefore, in Portuguese territory). Under his leadership, twelve thousand Indians set out upon a mournful anabasis: four thousand survivors reached the Paraná. In one village, Montoya counted 170 families, or, at the lowest estimate, a population of 800 to 850 persons.

These diverse facts, which cover nearly a century (from 1537 with the Conquistadors to 1631 with the Jesuits), and these figures, though they are roughly approximate, define, when joined to the Tupi figures, one and the same order of magnitude. Anchieta, Montoya's opposite number in Brazil, writes that in 1560 the society of Jesus had already brought under its guardianship eighty thousand Indians. This demographic homogeneity of the Tupi-Guarani calls for two tentative conclusions. The first is that, for these Indians, it is necessary to accept the high estimates. (I mean high in comparison with the usual rates of other indigenous societies.)

The second is that, when need be, we can legitimately make use of the Tupi figures for discussing the Guarani reality, provided we demonstrate – and that is what we shall attempt to do – the validity of our method.

Hence, let it be the Guarani population whose size we want to calculate. It is first of all a matter of determining the area of the territory occupied by these Indians. Unlike the Tupi habitat, which is impossible to measure, the task here is relatively easy, even if it does not permit us to obtain the precise results of a cadastral survey. The Guarani homeland was roughly bounded to the West by the Paraguay River, that is, by that part of its course which is situated between the 22nd parallel upstream and the 28th downstream. The southern frontier was located a little to the south of the junction of the Paraguay and the Paraná. The shores of the Atlantic constituted the eastern boundary, approximately from the Brazilian port of Paranagua to the north (the 26th parallel) to the present Uruguay border, formerly the homeland of the Charrua Indians (the 33rd parallel). One thus has two parallel lines (the course of the Paraguay and the seacoast) so that all we have to do is link their ends to discover the northern and southern boundaries of the Guarani territory. These boundaries correspond almost exactly to the furthest expansion of the Guarani. This quadrilateral of around 500,000 square kilometers was not wholly occupied by the Guarani, since other tribes lived in the region, mainly the Caingang. We can estimate the area of Guarani territory at 350,000 square kilometers.

Assuming this to be true, and knowing the *mean* density of the local groups, can we determine the total population? We would have to establish the number of local groups within the boundaries of the territory. Obviously, at this level our calculations are concerned with averages, "round" figures, and the results will be hypothetical, which does not mean they are arbitrary.

For this period – so far as we know – there only exists a single population census for the given territory. It is the one taken at the beginning of the seventeenth century by Father Claude d'Abbeville on the Island of Maranhão, during the last French attempt to colonize Brazil. Spread over this area of 1,200 square kilometers, 12,000 Tupi Indians were divided into 27 local groups, which gives an average of 450 persons per village occupying an average area of 45 square kilometers. Thus, the density of the population on the Island of Maranhão was exactly 10 inhabitants per square kilometer.

It is not possible to carry this density over to the Guarani land area (which would yield 3,500,000 Indians). Not that such a figure would alarm us, but the situation on Maranhão cannot be generalized. It was actually a zone of refuge for the Tupinamba who wanted to escape the Portuguese; consequently, the island was overpopulated. Paradoxically, that doubtless explains the small size of the groups: there were too many villages. In the coastal zone in the vicinity of the island, the French missionaries had counted 15 to 20 groups at Tapuytapera, 15 to 20 groups at Comma, and 20 to 24 groups among the Caité. There we have a total of 50 to 64 groups, which must have assembled between 30,000 and 40,000 individuals. And, according to the chroniclers, every one of these villages, dispersed over a much vaster area than that of the island, was more populous than those of the island. In short, the Island of Maranhão, given the density of its population, is a somewhat aberrant case, not usable for our purpose.

Very fortunately, we find in the chroniclers a priceless piece of information coming from Staden. During the 12 months that this man was a prisoner of the Tupinamba and trailed along from group to group, he had ample time to observe the life of his masters. He notes that in general the villages were separated by a distance of 9 to 12 kilometers, which would give around 150 square kilometers per local group. Let us keep this figure in mind and suppose that the same held true among the Guarani. It is now possible to find the number – albeit hypothetical and statistical – of Guarani local groups. It would amount to 350,000 divided by 150, or about 2,340. Let us agree on 600 persons as a credible average number per unit. We would then have: 2,340 x 600 = 1,404,000 inhabitants. Hence, nearly a million and a half Guarani Indians before the arrival of the whites. That implies a density of four inhabitants per square kilometer. (On the Island of Maranhão it was 10 inhabitants per square kilometer.)

This figure will appear enormous, improbable, inadmissable to some, if not to many. And yet, not only is there no reason (except ideological) to reject it, but I think our estimate is very modest. This is the point at which to cite the studies of what is called the Berkeley School, a group of demographic historians whose work overturns from top to bottom the classic certainties regarding America and its population. Pierre Chaunu[5] deserves the credit for having called to the attention of researchers, as early as 1960, the extreme importance of the discoveries made by the Berkeley School. I refer to two texts in which he presents a clear and closely reasoned statement of the method and results of the American investigators.

I will simply say that their demographic studies, conducted with irreproachable strictness, lead us to admit population figures and density rates heretofore unsuspected and bordering on the incredible. Thus, for the Mexican region of Anahuac (514,000 square kilometers), Borah and Cook decide upon a population of 25 million in 1519, that is, in Chaunu's words, "a density, comparable to France in 1789, of 50 inhabitants per square kilometer." This means that

5. "Une Histoire hispano-americaine pilote. En marge de l'oeuvre de l'École de Berkeley," *Revue historique*, vol. IV (1960), pp. 339-68. And: "La Population de l'Amérique indienne. Nouvelles recherches," *Revue historique*, vol. I (1963), p. 118.

as it progresses the demography of Berkeley, not hypothetical like ours, but proven, tends to confirm the highest figures. The recent work of Nathan Wachtel, dealing with the Andes, also establishes population rates in that area much higher than were thought possible: 10 million Indians in the Inca Empire in 1530. The necessary conclusion, then, is that the research conducted in Mexico and the Andes obliges us to accept the high estimates regarding the indigenous population of America. And that is why our figure of 1,500,000 Guarani Indians, absurd in the eyes of classic demography (Rosenblatt and company), becomes quite reasonable when placed in the demographic perspective traced by the Berkeley School.

If we are right, if 1,500,000 Guarani Indians did in fact inhabit a territory of 350,000 square kilometers, then it is necessary to radically transform our notions about the economic life of forest peoples (note the stupidity of the concept of subsistence economy), throw out the foolish beliefs about the purported inability of that type of agriculture to sustain a substantial population, and totally rethink the question of political power. I would point out that nothing prevented the Guarani from having a large population. In fact, let us consider the amount of cultivated space necessary. It is known that around half a hectare is required for a family of four or five persons. This figure is solidly established by the very precise measurements of Jacques Lizot[6] among the Yanomami; he discovered among them (at least as regards the groups in which he made his survey) an average of 1,070 square meters cultivated per person. Hence, if half a hectare is required for five persons, 150,000 hectares will have to be planted for 1,500,000 persons, that is, 1,500 square kilometers. This amounts to saying that the total area of the land cultivated at one time in order to meet the needs of 1,500,000 Indians takes up only 1/220th of the total territory. (On

6. Information personally communicated by Lizot.

the Island of Maranhão, a special case, as we have seen, the gardens still occupied only 1/90th of the surface of the island. And, according to Yves d'Evreux and Claude d'Abbeville, it did not appear that the island's twelve thousand inhabitants were especially threatened with food shortages.) Consequently, our figure of 1,500,000 Guarani, hypothetical though it is, is not improbable in the slightest. On the contrary, it is Rosenblatt's estimates that appear preposterous to me, seeing that he concludes there were 280,000 Indians in Paraguay in 1492. What he bases his calculations on is a mystery. As for Steward, he discovers a density of 28 inhabitants per 100 square kilometers for the Guarani, which should result in a total of 98,000 Indians. Why then does he decide that there were 200,000 in 1500? Such is the mystery and the inconsistency of "classic" Amerindian demography.

I am not forgetting that our own figure remains hypothetical (although one might consider the possibility of having established a population scale bearing no relation to previous calculations a success). Now, we have available a means of checking the validity of our calculations. The use of *the regression method*, brilliantly illustrated by the Berkeley School, will serve as a counter-verification to the method that correlated land surfaces with densities.

In fact, it is possible for us to proceed in a different way: based on the rate of depopulation. We have the good fortune to possess two estimates made by the Jesuits dealing with the Indian population grouped within the Missions, that is, with the virtual entirety of the Guarani. We owe the first to Father Sepp. He writes that in 1690 there were thirty réductions in all, none of which harbored fewer than six thousand Indians, and several having more than eight thousand inhabitants. Hence, at the end of the seventeenth century, there were around two hundred thousand Guarani (not counting the tribes that were free). The second estimate involves a genuine census, to the last unit, of all the inhabitants of the Missions. It is Father Lozano, the historian of the Society of Jesus, who sets forth the results in his irreplaceable *Historia de la Conquista del Paraguay*. The population was 130,000 persons in 1730. Let us consider this data.

As is shown by the disappearance, in less than a half-century, of more than a third of the population, the Jesuit Missions afforded the Indians residing within them scant protection against depopulation. Quite the contrary, the concentration of people in what grew to the size of small towns must have offered a choice medium for the spread of epidemics. The letters of the Jesuits are strewn with horrified disclosures concerning the ravages of smallpox and influenza. Father Sepp, for example, states that in 1687 an epidemic killed two thousand Indians *in a single Mission*, and that in 1695 a smallpox epidemic decimated *all the réductions*. It is quite evident that the depopulation process did not begin at the end of the seventeenth century, but as soon as the whites arrived, in the mid-sixteenth century. Father Lozano takes note of this: at the time of his writing the *Historia*, the Indian population had been drastically reduced, compared with the population prior to the Conquest. Thus he writes that at the end of the sixteenth century there were, in the region of Asunción alone, 24,000 *encomienda* Indians. In 1730, there were only 2,000 left. All the tribes that inhabited that part of Paraguay not under the authority of the Jesuits completely disappeared on account of *encomienda* slavery and epidemics. And, full of bitterness, Lozano writes: "The province of Paraguay was the most populated of the Indes and today it is nearly deserted; one finds there only those of the Missions."

The Berkeley investigators have plotted the depopulation curve for the Anahuac region. It is appalling, since of 25 million Indians in 1500, there were no more than a million left in 1605. Wachtel[7]

7. N. Wachtel, *La Vision des vaincus*, Paris, Gallimard, 1971.

cites figures for the Inca Empire that are scarcely less overwhelming: 10 million Indians in 1530, 1 million in 1600. For various reasons, the drop in population was less drastic than in Mexico, since the population was reduced by only (if it can be so stated) nine-tenths, whereas in Mexico it was reduced by 96/100ths. In both the Andes and Mexico, one witnesses a slow demographic recovery of the Indians, beginning with the end of the seventeenth century. This was not the case with the Guarani, since between 1690 and 1730 the population went from 200,000 to 130,000.

It can be estimated that in this period, the free Guarani, that is, those having escaped both the *encomienda* and the Missions, were no more than 20,000. Added to the 130,000 Guarani of the Missions, one obtains a total, then, of 150,000 in about 1730. Moreover, I am of the opinion that a relatively low rate of depopulation, compared with the Mexican example, should be accepted, of nine-tenths in two centuries (1530–1730). Consequently, the 150,000 Indians were ten times more numerous two centuries before, i.e., there were 1,500,000. I consider the rate of decline to be moderate, even though it is catastrophic. There appears in this a comparatively "protective" function of the Missions, in view of the fact the *encomienda* Indians disappeared at a faster rate: 24,000 at the end of the fifteenth century, 2,000 in 1730.

Obtained in this way, the figure of 1,500,000 Guarani in 1539 is no longer hypothetical as in the previous mode of calculation. I even think of it as a minimum. At all events, the convergence of the results obtained by the regression method and by the method of mean densities strengthens our conviction that we are not mistaken. We are a long way from the 250,000 Guarani in 1570, according to Rosenblatt, who thus admits a rate of depopulation of only 20 percent (250,000 Indians in 1570, 200,000 in 1650) for a period of almost a century. This rate is arbitrarily postulated and in complete contradiction with the rates established elsewhere throughout America. The thing becomes even more absurd with Steward: if there were 100,000 Guarani (given Steward's density of 28 inhabitants per square kilometer) in 1530, then this would be the only instance of a population showing a steady growth during the sixteenth and seventeenth centuries! It should not be taken seriously.

Hence, in order to theorize about the Guarani, it is necessary to accept these basic facts: *they numbered 1,500,000 before the Conquest, spread over 350,000 square kilometers, with a density of a little more than four inhabitants per square kilometer*. This estimate has significant implications.

(1) As regards the "demography" that can be deduced from the rough estimates of the chroniclers, it must be concluded that they were right. Their evaluations, all consistent with one another along the same scale of population, are equally consistent with the results obtained by our calculations. This discredits traditional demography by demonstrating its lack of scientific rigor. It makes one wonder why Rosenblatt, Steward, and Kroeber systematically opted – against the evidence – for the smallest possible size of the Indian population.

(2) As regards the question of political power, I will deal with it extensively at a later point. I will confine myself for the moment to the remark that between the leader of a band of Guayaki nomad hunters consisting of 25 to 30 persons, or the chief of a party of 100 warriors in the Chaco, and the great *mburuvicha*, the Tupi-Guarani leaders who led armies of several thousand men into combat, there is a radical difference, a difference in kind.

(3) But the essential point concerns the general question of Indian demography before the coming of the Whites. The research of the Berkeley School for Mexico and that of Wachtel for the Andes, in addition to converging in their results, have in common what they contribute to the so-called Highland cultures. Now, our mod-

est ideas on the Guarani, a forest people, moves – from the standpoint of its results – in the same direction as the works just alluded to: *for the peoples of the Forest, too, it is necessary* to adopt the higher population ratio. Hence, at this point I wish to affirm my agreement with P. Chaunu:

> The results of Borah and Cook lead to a complete revision of our perception of American history. It is no longer Dr. Rivet's 40 million men, a figure held to be excessive, that must be assumed for pre-Columbian America, but 80 and perhaps 100 million souls. The catastrophe of the Conquista ... was as great as Las Casas proclaimed it to be.

And this chilling conclusion: "it appears that one-fourth of mankind was annihilated by the microbic shocks of the sixteenth century."[8]

Our analysis of a very localized instance of forest dwellers ought to appear, if accepted, as a confirmation of the Berkeley hypotheses. It forces us to admit the higher demographic estimate for *all of America*, and not only for the Highland cultures. And this author will be more than content if this piece of work on the Guarani implies the conviction that it is essential "to undertake the great revision which the Berkeley School has been urging us to begin for the last 15 years."[9]

8. Pierre Chaunu, *L'Amérique et les Amériques*, Paris, A. Colin, 1964, p. 117.

9. Ibid., p. 118.

The Bow and the Basket

With almost no transition, night has taken hold of the forest, and the mass of great trees appears to move nearer. With the darkness also comes silence; the birds and monkeys are quiet and only the six dismal, forlorn notes of the *urutau* can be heard. And, as if by a tacit understanding with the general introversion that beings and things are preparing for, no further sound arises from this furtively inhabited space where a little group of men is camping. A band of Guayaki Indians has stopped here. Stirred up from time to time by a gust of wind, the reddish glow of six family fires extracts from the shadows the tenuous ring of palm branch shelters, the flimsy and transitory abode of the nomads, each one providing protection for a family in need of a resting place. The whispered conversations that followed the meal have gradually ceased; the women are sleeping, their arms still clasped around their curled-up children. One might think that the men had fallen asleep. But seated around their fire, keeping a mute and utterly motionless watch, they are not sleeping. Their thoughtful gaze, drawn to the neighboring darkness, shows a dreamy expectancy. For the men are getting ready to sing, and this evening, as sometimes happens at that auspicious hour, they will sing the hunter's song, each man singing separately: their meditation prepares them for the harmony of a soul and a moment that will find expression in the words to come. Soon a voice is raised up, almost imperceptible at first, coming as it does from within, a discreet murmur that refrains from enunciating anything distinct, for it is engaged in a patient search for just the right tone and the right discourse. But it rises by degrees, the singer is sure of himself now, and suddenly, the song rushes out, loud and free and strong. A second voice is stimulated and joins with the first, then another; words are uttered in quick succession, like answers always given in advance of the questions. All the men are singing now. They are still motionless, their gaze a little more lost than before; they all sing together, but each man sings his own song. They are masters of the night and each man means to be master of himself.

But without the knowledge of the Aché[1] [i.e., Guayaki] hunters, their hasty, fervent, earnest words come together in a dialogue they were intended to suppress.

A very noticeable opposition organizes and rules the everyday life of the Guayaki: the opposition of men and women. Their respective activities, characterized by a strict sexual division of tasks, constitute two distinctly separate domains. As with all Indian societies, these domains are complementary, but in contrast to the other societies, the Guayaki do not know any form of work in which both men and women take part. Agriculture, for instance, depends on masculine and feminine activities alike, since, while as a rule the women devote themselves to the sowing, the weeding of the gardens, and the harvesting of vegetables and grains, it is the men who occupy themselves with readying plots for planting by felling trees and burning off the dry vegetation. But although the roles are quite distinct and are never exchanged, they never-

1. Aché is the self-designation of the Guayaki.

theless ensure a common share in the realization and success of an enterprise as important as agriculture.

Now, nothing similar exists among the Guayaki. Being nomads ignorant of the art of planting, their economy is supported solely by exploiting the resources offered by the forest. These come under two main headings: the yield from hunting and the yield from gathering, the latter including most notably honey, larvae, and the pith of the pindo palm. One might think that the search for these two classes of food conformed to the widespread South American model whereby the men do the hunting, which is only natural, leaving the job of gathering to the women. In reality, things are done quite differently among the Guayaki, since the men do the hunting and the gathering *too*. Not that they would show more concern for the leisure activities of their spouses by exempting them from the duties that would normally be expected of them; but, in fact, the yield from gathering is obtained only at the expense of painful operations that the women could not accomplish without great difficulty: the location of the bee hives, the extraction of honey, the felling of trees, etc. What is involved, then, is a type of gathering that properly belongs in the category of masculine activities. Or, in other words, the gathering practiced elsewhere in America and consisting of the collecting of berries, fruits, roots, insects, and so on, is practically non-existent among the Guayaki, for the forest they occupy hardly abounds in resources of that sort. Hence, if the women do scarcely any collecting, this is because there is virtually nothing to collect.

The economic possibilities of the Guayaki being culturally limited by the absence of agriculture and naturally limited by the relative scarcity of edible plant life, it follows that the task of searching for the group's food provisions, begun anew each day, falls essentially to the men. In addition to their function – a crucial one for nomads – of transporting the family belongings, the hunters' wives do the basketry and pottery and make the strings for the bows; they do the cooking, take care of the children, and so forth. It turns out, then, that the women, far from being idle, devote their entire time to the execution of all these necessary labors. But it remains true nonetheless that the completely minor part played by the women in the basic area of food "production" leaves the men the engrossing and prestigious monopoly of it. Or, more precisely, the difference between the men and the women at the level of economic life can be understood as the opposition of a group of producers and a group of consumers.

As will be seen, Guayaki thought expresses clearly the nature of this opposition which, because it is situated at the very root of the social life of the tribe, dominates the economy of its everyday existence and gives meaning to a set of attitudes into which the web of social relations is woven. The space of nomad hunters cannot have the same dividing lines as that of sedentary agriculturists. The latter is structured into concentric circles, with a division between a cultural space comprised of the village and gardens, and a natural space occupied by the surrounding forest. In contrast, the Guayaki space is continually homogeneous, reduced to a pure extension in which the difference between nature and culture is seemingly done away with. But in reality the opposition already brought to light on the material plane of life furnishes the principle of a spatial dichotomy as well, one that is no less pertinent for being more concealed than is the case in societies belonging to a different cultural level. Among the Guayaki there exists a masculine space and a feminine space, defined respectively by the forest where the men do their hunting, and the encampment where the women reign. It is true that the layovers are very temporary: they rarely last more than three days. But they are the place of repose where the food prepared by the women is consumed, whereas the forest is the place of movement, the place especially consecrated to the excursions of men bent on finding game. It should not be inferred, of course, that the women are any less nomadic than the men. But owing to the type of economy on which hangs the existence of the tribe, the true masters of the forest are the men: they invest it in a real way, compelled as they are to explore its every detail in order to systematically exploit all its resources. For the men, the forest is a dangerous space, a space of risks, of ever renewed adventure, but for the women it is, on the contrary, a space passed through between two stops, a monotonous and tiresome crossing, a simple neutral expanse. At the opposite pole, the encampment offers the hunter the tranquillity of rest and the chance to do his routine handiwork, whereas for the women it is the place where their specific activities are carried out and where family life unfolds under their primary supervision. The forest and the encampment are thus allotted contrary signs depending on whether it is the men or the women who are the reference point. It might be said that the space of the "daily routine" is the forest for the women, the encampment for the men: for the latter, existence only becomes authentic when they give it concrete reality as hunters, that is, in the forest; and for the women, when, ceasing to be a means of transport, they are able to live in the encampment as wives and mothers.

Hence the value and scope of the socio-economic opposition between men and women can be gauged insofar as it structures the time and space of the Guayaki. Now, they do not allow the actual experience of this *praxis* to remain outside of thought: they have a clear awareness of it and the disequilibrium of the economic relations is expressed in the thinking of these Indians as the *opposition of the bow and the basket*. Each of these two instruments is in fact the medium, the sign, and the summary of one of two "styles" of existence that are at the same time opposed and carefully kept separate. It is hardly necessary to stress that the bow, the hunters' only weapon, is strictly a masculine tool, and that the basket, the women's consummate object, is used only by them: the men hunt, the women carry. In the main, Guayaki pedagogy is founded on this great separation of roles. Scarcely having reached the age of four or five, the little boy receives from his father a little bow that matches his size; from that moment he will begin to practice the art of shooting the arrow. A few years later, he is given a much larger bow, this time with effective arrows, and the birds he brings back to his mother are proof that he is a responsible boy and the promise that he will be a good hunter. When a few more years have gone by it is time for the initiation; the lower lip of the young man of about 15 is perforated, he gains the right to wear the labial ornament, the *beta*, and he is now looked upon as a true hunter, a *kybuchuété*. This signifies that in a short while he will be able to take a wife and consequently will have to supply the needs of a new household. His first concern, therefore, is to make himself a bow; henceforth a "productive" member of the band, he will hunt with a weapon shaped by his hands and nothing but death or old age will separate him from his bow. The woman's lot is complementary and parallel. The nine- or ten-year-old little girl receives from her mother a miniature basket, the making of which she has followed with rapt attention. Doubtless she carries nothing inside, but the gratuitous posture she assumes while walking, her head lowered and her neck straining in anticipation of its effort to come, prepares her for a future that is very near. For the appearance of her first menstruation, around the age of 12 or 13, and the ritual that ratifies the advent of womanhood make the young woman into a *daré*, a woman soon to be the wife of a hunter. As the first task required by her new status, and the mark of her definitive condition, she then makes her own basket. And each of the two, the young man and the young woman, master and prisoner, thus gains entry into adulthood. In the end, when the hunter dies, his bow and arrows are ritually buried, as is the woman's last basket: for, being the very signs of the persons, they cannot outlive them.

The Guayaki experience the effects of this great opposition, on which the operation of their society depends, through a system of reciprocal prohibitions: one forbids the women to touch the hunter's bow, the other keeps the men from handling the basket. Generally speaking, the tools and instruments are sexually neuter, so to speak: men and women alike can make use of them. This taboo with respect to physical contact with the most palpable emblems of the opposite sex thus makes it possible to avoid any transgression of the socio-sexual order that governs the life of the group. It is scrupulously respected, and one never witnesses the bizarre meeting of a woman and a bow, nor, too ludicrous to imagine, that of a hunter and a basket. The feelings evoked in each of the sexes relative to the privileged object of the other sex are very different: a hunter could not bear the shame of carrying a basket, whereas his wife would be afraid to touch his bow. This is because contact between a woman and a bow is much more serious than that between a man and a basket. If a woman were to take it upon herself to lay hold of a bow, she would certainly bring down on its owner the *pané*, that is, bad luck at hunting, which would be disastrous for the Guayaki economy. As for the hunter, the thing he sees in the basket and shrinks from is precisely the potential threat of what he fears above all else, the *pané*. For whenever a man falls victim to this veritable curse, being unable to perform his hunter's function, he loses his own nature by that very fact, he is drained of his substance: forced to abandon a now useless bow, there is nothing left for him but to forfeit his masculinity and, a tragic and resigned figure, take up a basket. The harsh law of the Guayaki leaves them no way out. The men have no existence except as hunters, and they remain secure in their being by preserving their bow from the contact of women. Conversely, if an individual no longer manages to realize himself as a hunter, at the same time he ceases to be a man. Going from the bow to the basket, metaphorically he *becomes a woman*. As a matter of fact, the conjunction of the man and the bow cannot be broken without changing into its complementary opposite: that of the woman and the basket.

Now the logic of this closed system, made up of four terms grouped into two opposite pairs, was actually fulfilled: among the Guayaki there were two men who carried baskets. One, named Chachubutawachugi, was *pané*. He did not possess a bow and the only hunting he occasionally indulged in was the capture, by hand, of armadillos and coatis. Although this type of hunting is commonly practiced by all the Guayaki, it is far from being regarded by them as having the same dignity as bow hunting, the *jyvondy*. Added to this was the circumstance that Chachubutawachugi was a widower; and since he was *pané* no woman would have anything to do with him, not even as a secondary husband. Nor did he try to be integrated into the family of one of his relatives: the latter would have found the continual presence of a man, whose technical incompetence was aggravated by an excellent appetite, undesirable. Without a bow and hence without a wife, he had no further choice but to accept his sad lot. He never accompanied the other men on their hunting expeditions, but went off alone, or in the company of women, to look for the larvae, honey, or fruit he had spotted previously. And in order to carry the results of his gathering, he toted a basket which a woman had given to him as a present. His access to women barred by bad luck at hunting, he lost, in part at least, his manly quality and thus found himself relegated to the symbolic field of the basket.

The second instance is slightly different. Krembegi was in fact a sodomite. He lived as a woman in the midst of women, as a rule wearing his hair conspicuously longer than the other men, and only doing a woman's work: he knew how to "weave" and from the animal teeth the hunters gave him he made bracelets that demonstrated an artistic taste and aptitude that were much more pronounced than in the things made by the women. And finally, he was of course the owner of a basket. In brief, Krembegi thus testified to the existence within Guayaki culture of a refinement ordinarily reserved for less rustic societies. This incomprehensible pederast conceived of himself as a woman and had adopted the attitudes and behavior peculiar to that sex. For example, he would refuse the contact of a bow with as much conviction as a hunter would that of a basket; he considered his rightful place to be the world of women. Krembegi was homosexual because he was *pané*. Perhaps his bad luck at hunting also stemmed from his being previously an unconscious invert. At any rate, the confidential asides of his companions let it be known that his homosexuality had become official, that is, socially recognized, when it became apparent that he was incapable of using a bow: to the Guayaki themselves, he was a *kyrypy-meno* (anus-make love) because he was *pané*.

Moreover, the Aché maintained a quite different attitude towards each of the two basket carriers mentioned above. The first, Chachubutawachugi, was the butt of general ridicule, albeit free of real meanness. The men made light of him more or less openly, the women laughed behind his back, and the children respected him much less than the rest of the adults. Krembegi on the contrary attracted no special attention; his ineptness as a hunter and his homosexuality were deemed evident and taken for granted. Now and then certain hunters would make him their sexual partner, displaying in these erotic games more bawdiness – it would seem – than perversion. But this never resulted in any feeling of scorn for him on their part. Reciprocally, these two Guayaki showed themselves to be unevenly adapted to their new status, thus conforming to the image their own society created for them. Just as Krembegi was comfortable, placid, and serene in his role of a man become a woman, so Chachubutawachugi appeared anxious, nervous, and often discontent. What explains this difference, brought by the Aché into the treatment accorded two individuals who, at least in formal terms, were *negatively* identical? The explanation is that, while they both occupied the same position in relation to the other men in that they were both *pané*, their positive status ceased to be equivalent because one, Chachubutawachugi, although forced to give up in part his masculine attributes, had remained a man, whereas the other, Krembegi, had gone so far as to assume the ultimate consequences of his condition as a non-hunting man by "becoming" a woman. Or, in other words, the latter's homosexuality had permitted him to find the topos he was logically consigned to by his unfitness to occupy the space of men; in return, the other man, refusing the movement of the same logic, was expelled from the circle of the men, but without being assimilated into that of the women. This meant that, consequently, *he literally was nowhere*, and that he was in a much more uncomfortable situation than Krembegi. In the eyes of the Aché, the latter occupied a well defined, though paradoxical place; as his position in the group was in a sense uncompromised by any ambiguity, it came out as normal, even if this new norm was that of women. Chachubutawachugi, on the other hand, constituted in his very person a kind of logical scandal. Because he was not situated in any clearly defined place, he evaded the system and introduced an element of disorder into it: from a certain viewpoint it could be said that the abnormal was none other than he. Whence no doubt the secret aggressiveness of the Guayaki towards him that sometimes could be detected underneath the derision. Whence too, more than likely, the psychological difficulties he was experiencing, and an acute feeling of abandonment: that is how difficult it is to maintain the absurd conjunction of a man and a basket. Pathetically, Chachubutawachugi tried to remain a man without being a hunter: he thus lay himself open to ridicule and jeers, for he was the point of contact between two areas that are normally separate.

It is logical to assume that these two men preserved with respect to their baskets the difference in the relationships they entertained with their masculinity. As a matter of fact Krembegi carried his basket like the women, that is, with the headband *round his forehead*. As for Chachubutawachugi, he passed the same bandeau *round his chest* and never round his forehead. This was a notoriously uncomfortable way of carrying a basket, more tiring than any other; but for him it was also the only means of showing that, even without a bow, he was still a man.

Central in its position and powerful in its effects, the great opposition of men and women thus puts its stamp on all aspects of Guayaki life. It is again this opposition that underlies the difference between the singing of the men and that of the women. The masculine *prerä* and the feminine *chengaruvara* in fact are total opposites in style and content. They express two modes of existence, two presences in the world, two value systems that are quite different from one another. Then again, one can scarcely speak of singing where the women are concerned; it is really a matter of a generalized "tearful salutation": even when they are not ritually greeting a stranger or a relative who has been absent for a long while, the women "sing" while weeping. In a plaintive tone, but loud voices, squatting with their faces hidden by their hands, they punctuate every phrase with their chant composed of strident sobbing. Often all the women sing together and the din created by their concerted wailing exerts on the unwitting listener an impression of malaise. One's surprise is only increased by the sight of the weepers' calm faces and dry eyes when everything is over. It is appropriate to note in addition that the women's singing always occurs on ritual occasions; either during the principal ceremonies of Guayaki society, or by taking advantage of the many opportunities provided by everyday life. For example, a hunter brings some animal into the camp: a woman "greets" it by crying because it calls to mind some departed relative; or again, if a child hurts himself while playing, his mother immediately breaks into a *chengaruvara* exactly like all the others. The women's singing is never joyful, as one might expect. The themes of the songs are always death, illness, and the violence of the whites, and the women thus take upon themselves all the pain and all the anguish of the Aché.

The contrast it forms to the singing of the men is startling. It seems that among the Guayaki there exists a sort of sexual division of linguistic labor in keeping with which all the negative aspects of existence are taken over by the women, whereas the men dedicate themselves to celebrating, if not the pleasures of existence, at least the values that make it bearable. While in her very gestures the woman hides and appears to humble herself in order to sing, or rather weep, the hunter, on the contrary, with head held high and body straight, glorifies himself in his song. His self-assurance asserts itself in the extreme virility the hunter brings to his singing, a harmony with oneself that nothing can deny. The language of the masculine song, moreover, is highly distorted. As its improvisation becomes progressively more fluent and rich, as the words flow out effortlessly, the singer subjects them to such a radical transformation that after a while one would think he were hearing another language: for a non-Aché, these songs are strictly incomprehensible. With regard to their thematic composition, it basically consists of an emphatic praise which the singer directs at himself. In point of fact, the content of his discourse is strictly personal and everything in it is said in the first person. The men speak almost exclusively of their exploits as hunters, of the animals they have encountered, the injuries they have received, their skill at shooting arrows. This is a leitmotif that is repeated indefinitely, and one hears it proclaimed in a manner that is almost obsessional: *cho rö bretete, cho rö jyvondy, cho rö yma wachu, yma chija* ("I am a great hunter, I am in the habit of killing with my arrows, I am a powerful nature, a nature incensed and aggressive!"). And often, as if to indicate how indisputable his glory is, he punctuates his phrase by extending it with a vigorous *cho, cho, cho* ("me, me, me").[2]

The difference in the songs admirably conveys the opposition of the sexes. The women's song is a lament that is most frequently choral, nearly always heard during the day; that of the men nearly always bursts forth at night, and while their sometimes simultaneous voices can give the impression of a choir, this is a false appearance, because each singer is actually a soloist. Furthermore, the feminine *chengaruvara* appears to consist of mechanically repeated formulas adapted to the various ritual circumstances. In contrast, the *prerä* of the hunters depends only on their mood and is organized solely in terms of their individuality. It is a purely personal improvisation that permits a search for artistic effects in the play of the voice. Thus the collective quality of the women's singing and individual quality of the men's refers us back to the opposition we started from: as the only truly "productive" element of Guayaki society, the hunters experience a creative freedom in the domain of language that their position as "consumer group" denies the women.

Now this freedom lived and expressed by the men as hunters is not just a token of the nature of the relationship whereby the men as a group are tied to the women and set apart from them. For, through the men's singing, a second, secret opposition is uncov-

2. As might be expected, the two *pané* men just referred to maintained very different attitudes towards the singing: Chachubutawachugi sang only during certain ceremonies calling for his direct participation, for instance, the birth of a child. Krembegi never sang.

ered, this one no less powerful than the first but unconscious: *the opposition of the hunters among themselves*. And in order to better listen to their song and truly understand what it is saying, we must go back once again to the ethnology of the Guayaki and the basic dimensions of their culture.

For the Aché hunter there is an alimentary taboo that categorically forbids him to consume the meat of his own kill: *bai jyvombré ja uemere* ("The animals one has killed must not be eaten by oneself."). So that when a man arrives at the encampment he divides the product of his hunt between his family (wife and children) and the other members of the band; naturally, he will not partake of the meat prepared by his wife. Now, as we have seen, game occupies the most important place in the Guayaki diet. The result is that every man will spend his life hunting for the others' benefit and receiving from them his own nourishment. This prohibition is scrupulously honored, even by the boys when they kill birds. One of the most important consequences is that necessity prevents the Indians from scattering in elementary families: unless he gave up the taboo, the man would die of hunger. This makes it necessary to move in a group. To account for this, the Guayaki hold that eating the animals killed by oneself is the surest way to draw the *pané* down upon oneself. This major fear of the hunters is sufficient to impose respect for the prohibition it establishes: if one wants to continue killing animals, one must not eat them. The indigenous theory is simply based on the idea that the conjunction between the hunter and dead animals in the sphere of consumption would be followed by a disjunction between the hunters and living animals in the sphere of "production." Hence its thrust is essentially negative since it resolves into the forbidding of that conjunction.

In reality, this food taboo also possesses a positive value in that it operates as a structural principle which forms the very basis of

Guayaki society. By setting up a negative relation between each Guayaki hunter and the product of his hunt, it places *all* the men in the same position relative to one another, and the reciprocity of the gift of food reveals itself to be not only possible but imperative: every hunter is at the same time a giver and a taker of meat. The taboo regarding game appears, then, as the founding act of the exchange of food among the Guayaki, that is, as the foundation of their society itself. Other societies no doubt are acquainted with this same taboo. But among the Guayaki it assumes an especially great importance from the fact that it relates precisely to their main source of nourishment. By compelling the individual to part with his own game, it obliges him to place trust in others, thus allowing the social tie to be joined in a definitive way. The interdependence of the hunters guarantees the solidity and permanence of that tie, and the society gains in strength what the individuals lose in autonomy. The disjunction of the hunter and his game establishes the conjunction of the hunters among themselves, that is, the contract that governs Guayaki society. Furthermore, the disjunction in the sphere of consumption between hunters and dead animals, by protecting the former from the *pané*, ensures the future repetition of the conjunction between hunters and living animals, that is, success at hunting and, consequently, the survival of society.

By banishing direct contact between the hunter and his own game to the realm of Nature, the alimentary taboo places itself at the heart of Culture: it interposes the mediation of the other hunters between the hunter and his food supply. Thus we see the exchange of game, which in large measure circumscribes economic life among the Guayaki, transform each individual hunter, by virtue of its restraining character, into a *relation*. The treacherous space of prohibition and transgression lies deep between the hunter and his "product"; the fear of the *pané* lays the foundation for exchange by depriving the hunter of any right to his own game: he only has a right to the game of others. Now, it is striking to discover that this same relational structure whereby the men are strictly defined at the level of the circulation of goods is repeated in the domain of matrimonial institutions.

As early as the beginning of the sixteenth century, the first Jesuit missionaries had tried, in vain, to make contact with the Guayaki. They were able, however, to gather a large amount of information about that mysterious tribe, and they learned in this way, to their great surprise, that, contrary to what occurred among the other savages, among the Guayaki there was a preponderance of men over women. They were not mistaken, for, nearly 400 years after them, I was able to observe the same disequilibrium in the sex ratio: in one of the two southern groups, for instance, there was exactly one woman for every two men. There is no need to look into the causes of this anomaly here,[3] but it is important to examine the consequences of it. No matter what type of marriage is preferred by a society, there is always about the same number of potential wives as husbands. The Guayaki society had a choice among several solutions for equalizing these two numbers. To begin with, since the suicidal solution of abandoning the incest prohibition was not possible, the society could have engaged in male infanticide. But every male child is a future hunter, that is, an essential member of the community: hence it would have been contradictory to get rid of them. It also would have been possible to accept the existence of a relatively large number of bachelors; but this choice would have been even more risky than the first because in societies as demographically reduced as this one, there is nothing more dangerous to the equilibrium of the group than a bachelor. So, instead of artificially diminishing the number of possible

3. Pierre Clastres, *Chronique des Indiens Guayaki*, Paris, Plon, 1972.

husbands, nothing remained but to increase the number of actual husbands each woman could have, that is, institute a system of polyandric marriage. And in point of fact, the entire surplus of men is absorbed by the women in the form of secondary husbands, *japetyva*, who will occupy a place beside the shared wife nearly as enviable as that of the *imété* or principal husband.

Thus Guayaki society was able to preserve itself from a mortal danger by adapting the conjugal family to this completely unbalanced demography. What does that imply from the men's standpoint? Virtually none of them can conjugate his wife in the singular, so to speak, since he is not the only husband and shares with one and sometimes even two other men. One might think that, in view of its being the cultural norm in and by which the men define themselves, this situation would not affect them and they would not react to it in any especially pronounced way. In actual fact, the relationship between the culture and the individuals in whom it is embodied is not mechanical, and the Guayaki husbands, while they accept the only possible solution to the problem confronting them, have difficulty in resigning themselves to it nonetheless. The polyandric households lead a tranquil existence no doubt, and the three elements of the conjugal triangle live in mutual respect. That does not alter the fact that the men almost always harbor – for they never talk about it between themselves – feelings of irritation, not to say aggressiveness towards the co-proprietor of their wife. In the course of my stay among the Guayaki, a married woman became involved in a love affair with a young bachelor. The furious husband first lashed out at his rival, then, upon the insistence and the blackmail of his wife, he finally agreed to make the situation legal by allowing the clandestine lover to become the official secondary husband to his spouse. For that matter, he had no choice; if he had refused this arrangement, his wife might have deserted him, thereby condemning him to celibacy, as there was no other available woman in the tribe. Moreover, group pressure, concerned about eliminating any disruptive elements, sooner or later would have compelled him to conform to an institution meant precisely to solve this sort of problem. He resigned himself, therefore, to sharing his wife with another, but entirely against his will. At about the same time, the secondary husband of another woman died. His relations with the principal husband had always been good: marked if not by an extreme cordiality, at least by an unfailing courtesy. But the surviving *imété* still did not appear to be especially heartbroken to see the *japetyva* pass on. He did not conceal his satisfaction:"I am pleased," he said, "now I am my wife's only husband."

More examples of this kind could be cited, but the two cases just alluded to suffice to show that while Guayaki men accept polyandry, they are far from feeling at ease with it. There is a sort of "gap" between this matrimonial institution that effectively protects the integrity of the group, and the individuals it affects.[4] The men approve of polyandry because it is necessary owing to the shortage of women, but they suffer it as a very disagreeable obligation. Many Guayaki husbands have to share their wife with another man, and as regards those who exercise their conjugal rights alone, they run the risk of seeing this rare and fragile monopoly terminated by the competition of a bachelor or widower. Guayaki husbands consequently play a mediating role between wife givers and wife takers, *and also* between the takers themselves.

4. Ten years or so before, a split had divided the Aché Gatu tribe. The wife of the chief was having extra-marital relations with a young man. The husband had grown very angry and broke off from the group, taking a part of the Guayaki along with him. He even threatened to massacre with arrows those who did not follow him. It was only after several months had passed that the fear of losing his wife and the collective pressure of the Aché Gatu led him to acknowledge his wife's lover as her *japetyva*.

The exchange through which a man gives his daughter or sister to another does not end the circulation – as it were – of that woman: the receiver of this "message" sooner or later will have to share the "reading" of it with another man. The exchange of women in itself is a maker of alliances between families; but polyandry in its Guayaki form superimposes itself on the exchange of women in order to fill a quite specific function: it makes it possible to preserve as a culture the social life that the group achieves through the exchange of women. Strictly speaking, marriage among the Guayaki can only be polyandric since only in this form does it acquire the value and the importance of an institution that is continually creating and maintaining the society as such. If the Guayaki were to reject polyandry, their society would not endure; being unable, due to their small numbers, to obtain women for themselves by attacking other tribes, they would face the prospect of a civil war between bachelors and possessors of wives, that is, a collective suicide of the tribe. In this way, polyandry suppresses the opposition occasioned by the scarcity of women.

Hence it is a kind of reason of State that determines Guayaki husbands to accept polyandry. Each of them forgoes the exclusive use of his spouse for the benefit of some bachelor of the tribe, so that the tribe can continue to exist as a social unit. By relinquishing one half of their matrimonial rights, Aché husbands make communal life and the survival of society possible. But, as the anecdotes reported above show, that does not prevent latent feelings of frustration and discontent from existing: one agrees in the end to share his wife with another because one cannot do otherwise, but this is done with obvious ill-humor. Every Guayaki man is a potential wife giver or wife receiver. Long before making up for the woman he has received by the daughter she will give him, he will have to offer another man his own wife without reciprocity being established, something that is not possible: the wife is given too, before the daughter. This means that among the Guayaki a man is a husband only by agreeing to be half a husband, and the superiority of the principal husband over the secondary husband does nothing to alter the fact that the first must take the rights of the second into account. It is not the personal relations between brothers-in-law that are most outstanding, but those between the husbands of the same wife and, as we have seen, they are most often negative.

Is it now possible to discern a structural analogy between the relationship of the hunter to his game and that of the husband to his wife? First, we observe that animals and wives occupy an equivalent position with regard to the man as hunter and as husband. In one case, the man finds himself radically separated from the product of his hunt, since he must not consume it; in the other, he is never completely a husband, he is no more than a half-husband at best: a third person comes between a man and his wife, namely the secondary husband. Hence, just as a man depends on the hunting of others for his own food, similarly in order to "consume" his wife,[5] a husband depends on the other husband, whose desires he must respect if co-existence is not to be rendered impossible. So the polyandric system doubly restricts the matrimonial rights of each husband: with reference to the men who neutralize each other, as it were, and with reference to the woman who, knowing full well how to profit from the situation, is not at a loss when it comes to dividing her husbands in order to extend her reign over them.

Consequently, from a formal viewpoint, game is to the hunter what the wife is to the husband, inasmuch as both have only a mediated relationship to the man: for every Guayaki hunter, the relationship to animal food and to women goes by way of other men. The very special circumstances of their life force the Guayaki

5. It is not a matter of a play on words: in Guayaki, the same word designates the act of feeding oneself and making love (*tyku*).

to allot exchange and reciprocity a coefficient of severity that is much greater than elsewhere, and the demands of this hyper-exchange are so oppressive as to weigh on the consciousness of the Indians and sometimes give rise to conflicts stemming from the necessity of polyandry. Actually, it should be noted that *for the male Indians themselves* the obligation to give away their game is by no means experienced as such, whereas sharing a wife is felt as alienation. But it is the *formal* identity of the twofold relation hunter-game and husband-wife that ought to be stressed here. The alimentary taboo and the shortage of women perform, each in its own sphere, parallel functions: safeguarding the existence of the society through the interdependence of the men, and insuring its continuation through the sharing of the women. Positive in the sense that they continually create and re-create the social structure itself, these functions are also coupled with a negative dimension in that they put between the man, on one side, his game and his wife, on the other, all the distance that inheres in the social field. It is here that the structural relation of man to the essence of the group is determined, that is, exchange. In fact, the gift of game and the sharing of wives refer respectively to two of the three main supports on which the cultural edifice rests: the exchange of goods and the exchange of women.

This twofold and identical relationship of men to their society, even though it never emerges in their consciousness, is not static, however. On the contrary, being all the more active for remaining unconscious, it is what defines the very singular relation of the hunters to the third order of reality: language as the exchange of messages. For, in their singing, the men express both the unthought knowledge of their lot as hunters and husbands, and their protest against that lot. In this manner, the complete configuration formed by the threefold connection of the men to exchange becomes clear: the individual hunter occupies its center while the symbolic world of goods, women, and words marks out its periphery. But while the relationship of the man to game and to women consists of a disjunction that founds society, his relationship to language condenses, in the song, into a conjunction that is sufficiently radical to negate precisely language's communicative function and, thereby, exchange itself. Consequently, the hunter's song assumes a position which is symmetrical to and the reverse of the food taboo and polyandry, and it shows by its form and its content that the men, as hunters and husbands, want to negate the latter.

It will be recalled that the content of the masculine songs is highly personal, always delivered in the first person, and strictly devoted to praising the singer in his capacity as a good hunter. Why is that the case? The men's song, while it is certainly language, is however no longer the ordinary language of everyday life, the language that enables the exchange of linguistic signs to take place. Indeed it is the opposite. If to speak is to transmit a message intended for a receiver, then the song of the Aché men is located outside language. For who listens to the hunter's song besides the hunter himself, and for whom is the message intended if not the very one who transmits it? Being himself the object and the subject of his song, the hunter dedicates its lyric recitative to himself alone. As prisoners of an exchange that makes them mere components of a system, the Guayaki long to free themselves from the requirements of that exchange, but they are powerless to reject it in the very domain in which they complete it and suffer its effects. Given this incapacity, how were they to eliminate the terms without severing the relations? Language was the only resource that offered itself to them. The Guayaki hunters found in their song the innocent and profound ruse that enables them to reject in the domain of language the exchange they are unable to abolish in the domain of goods and women.

It was certainly not an idle choice when the men decided on

the nocturnal solo of their song as the hymn of their freedom. It alone is capable of articulating an experience without which they would perhaps be unable to bear the constant tension which the necessities of social life impose on their everyday existence. Thus the song of the hunter, that endo-language, is for him the moment of his true repose in that it provides a refuge in which to experience the freedom of his *solitude*. That is why, once night has fallen, each man takes possession of the realm that is his own preserve, where, at peace with himself, at last he can dream through his words the impossible "private talk with oneself." But the Aché hunters, naked and savage poets who endow their language with a new sanctity, are unaware that in mastering the same magic of the word (are not their simultaneous songs the same *chanson de geste*, their own verse-chronicle?), the hope each has of asserting his difference vanishes. What does it matter in any case? When they sing it is, in their words, *ury vwä*, "to be content." And thus, one after another, hour upon hour, these defiant words are declaimed a hundred times: "I am a great hunter; I kill much with my arrows; I am a strong nature." But there is no one to take up the challenges that are hurled, and if the hunter's song gives him the arrogance of a victory, this is because it is meant as the forgetting of all combat. Let it be clear that no biology of culture is being suggested here; social life is not life itself and exchange is not a struggle. The observation of one primitive society shows us the contrary; while exchange as the essence of the social can take the dramatic form of a competition between those who exchange, this competition is doomed to remain static because the permanence of a "social contract" requires that there be neither victor nor vanquished and that the gains and losses balance out for both sides. In short, one might say that social life is a "combat" that precludes any victory. Conversely, if it becomes possible to speak of a "victory," this is because it concerns someone unfit, that is, outside social life. In the end, what the songs of the Guayaki Indians bring back to us is that it is impossible to win on all fronts, that one cannot but respect the rules of the social game, and that the fascination of non-participation entices one to a great illusion.

By their nature and their function, these songs illustrate in exemplary form the general relationship of man to language. These distant voices call on us to ponder that relationship; they invite us to follow a path that is now all but obliterated, and the thought of savages, the product of a still primal language, only motions in the direction of thought. We have seen, as a matter of fact, that beyond the contentment it obtains for them, their singing furnishes the hunters – and without their knowing it – the means to escape from social life by refusing the exchange that underlies it. The same movement by which the singer detaches himself from the *social* man he is induces him to know and declare himself as a concrete *individuality* utterly closed upon itself. The same man exists, then, as a pure *relation* in the sphere of the exchange of goods and women, and as a monad, so to speak, in the sphere of language. It is through the song that he comes to consciousness of himself as an *I* and thereby gains the legitimate usage of that personal pronoun. The man exists for himself in and through his particular song: I sing, therefore I am. Now it is quite evident that if language, in the guise of the song, is designated to the man as the true locus of his being, what is at issue is no longer language as the archetype of exchange, since that is precisely the thing he is trying to be free of. In other words, the very model of the world of communication is also the means of escaping that world. A word spoken can be both a message exchanged and the negation of all messages. It can be pronounced as a sign and as the opposite of a sign. Hence, the song of the Guayaki refers us to the essential and double nature of language, which unfolds sometimes in its open function of communication, other times in its closed function of constructing an Ego. This capacity of language to perform inverse functions rests on the possibility of its dividing in two: it is both *sign* and *value*.

Far from having the innocence of a hobby or mere diversion, the song of the Guayaki hunters announces the firm intent that is its motive force: to escape the subjection of man to the general network of signs (in this context, words are only the privileged metaphor for that network) by aggression against language in the form of a transgression of its function. What becomes of a spoken word when it is no longer used as a medium of communication, when it is diverted from its "natural" end, which is the relationship to the Other? Separated from their nature as signs, words are no longer intended for any listener; the words of the song are an end in themselves; for the one who utters them, they change into values. Moreover, by changing from a system of mobile signs between transmitters and receivers into a mere value position for an Ego, language does not thereby cease being the place where meaning is lodged: the meta-social is not the infra-individual, the hunter's solitary song is not the discourse of a madman, and his words are not so many cries. Meaning persists, detached from any message, and it is its absolute permanence that supplies the ground on which speech can stand as value and nothing else. Language can be language no longer without dissolving by that fact into senselessness, and anyone can understand the song of the Guayaki although nothing is stated therein. Or rather, what it bids us to understand is that speaking need not always engage another; that language can be wielded for itself, and that it is not confined to the function it performs: the Guayaki song is language reflected back on itself, abolishing the social world of signs in order to provoke the emergence of meaning as an absolute value. There is no paradox, then, in the fact that what is most unconscious and collective in man – his language – can also be his most transparent consciousness and his most liberated dimension. *To the disjunction of speech and signs in the song corresponds the disjunction of man and the social world for the singer*, and the conversion of meaning into value is the conversion of an individual into the *subject* of his solitude.

Man is a political animal; society does not amount to the sum of its individual members; and the difference between the addition it is not and the system that defines it consists in the exchange and reciprocity through which men are linked to one another. There would be no point in recalling these truisms if I did not mean to indicate that they suggest their contrary. To wit, if man is a "sick animal" this is because he is not solely a "political animal," and from his anxiety there awakens the great desire that obsesses him: the desire to escape a necessity that is dimly perceived as a destiny and cast aside the restraints of exchange, the desire to refuse his social being so as to rid himself of his *condition*. For it is indeed owing to man's awareness that he is traversed and borne along by the reality of the social that there originates the desire to be something more than that reality and the longing to get away from it. By listening attentively to the singing of a few savages we come to realize that what is involved in actual fact is a general song that gives voice to the universal dream of no longer being what one is.

Placed at the very heart of the human condition, the desire to have done with that condition is realized only as a dream that can be conveyed in manifold ways, sometimes in myth, sometimes, as with the Guayaki, in song. Perhaps the song of the Aché hunters is nothing else but their individual myth. At any rate, the men's secret desire proves its own impossibility in that they can do no more than dream it, and language is the only space in which it comes true. Now this close relationship between dreaming and speech, while it marks the failure of the men to repudiate what they are, signifies at the same time the triumph of language. In fact, language alone can accomplish the twofold mission of bringing the men together and breaking the ties that unite them. As the sole possibility for them to transcend their condition, it presents itself as their *beyond*, and words uttered for the *value* they possess are the province of the gods.

Despite appearances, it is still the song of the Guayaki to which we are listening. If there is any doubt, might this not be precisely because its language is no longer comprehensible to us? There is certainly no longer any question here of translation. All things considered, the song of the Aché hunters calls our attention to a certain kinship between man and his language: to be more exact, a kinship of a kind that seems to survive only in primitive man. This implies that, putting aside all notions of exoticism, the naive discourse of savages obliges us to reflect on the thing that poets and thinkers alone remember: that language is not simply an instrument, that man can be on a level with it, and that the modern West loses the sense of its value through the excessive wear it subjects it to. The language of civilized man has become completely *external* to him, for it is no longer anything for him but a pure means of communication and information. The quality of meaning and the quantity of signs vary in inverse ratio. Primitive cultures, on the contrary, more concerned to celebrate language than to put it to use, have been able to maintain that *internal* relationship with it that is already in itself an alliance with the sacred. For primitive man, there is no poetic language, for his language is already in itself a natural poem where dwells the value of words. And while I have spoken of the song of the Guayaki as an aggression against language, it should henceforth be understood as the shelter that protects him. But is it still possible to hear, from wretched wandering savages, the all too strong lesson concerning the proper usage of language?

Such is the life of the Guayaki Indians. By day they walk together through the forest, women and men, the bow in front, the basket behind. The coming of night separates them, each one surrendering to his dream. The women sleep and the hunters sometimes sing, alone. Pagans and barbarians, only death saves them from the rest.

What Makes Indians Laugh

Resolved to take the narratives of "savages" *seriously*, structural analysis has shown for some years that they are in fact quite serious; that they present a system of inquiries which raises mythical thinking to the level of thought as such. They have acquired a new prestige since the *Mythologiques* of Lévi-Strauss taught us that myths are not empty talk. And it is merely giving them their due to endow them with such gravity. Yet, perhaps the renewed interest aroused by myths will lead us this time to take them too "seriously," as it were, and to assess poorly their range of thought. In short, if their less stringent aspects are left obscure, a kind of mythomania may gain currency which ignores a trait a great number of myths have in common, one not incompatible with their gravity: their humor.

Serious both for those who relate them (the Indians, for instance) and those who record or read them, myths can nevertheless exhibit a comic intent. They sometimes perform the express function of amusing their listeners, triggering their mirth. If one cares about preserving the integral truth of myths, the real significance of the laughter they provoke must not be underestimated. The fact must be taken into account that a myth can *simultaneously* speak of serious things and set those who hear it laughing. Despite its harshness, the daily life of "primitives" is not always governed by toil and worry. They too indulge in real moments of relaxation, and their acute sense of the absurd frequently has them making fun of their own fears. Now it is not unusual for these cultures to entrust their myths with the job of entertaining the people by de-dramatizing, as it were, their existence.

The two myths we are about to read belong in that category. They were collected last year among the Chulupi Indians who live in the southern part of the Paraguayan Chaco. These narratives, going from the mock-heroic to the ribald, yet not altogether wanting in lyricism, are well known by all members of the tribe, young and old; but when they really want to laugh, they ask some old man versed in the traditional lore to tell these stories one more time. The effect never fails: the smiles at the beginning become chortles that are barely stifled, then shameless peals of laughter burst out, and finally it is all howls of joy. While these myths were being recorded on tape, the uproar of the dozens of Indians who were listening sometimes blotted out the voice of the narrator, who was himself constantly on the verge of losing his composure. We are not Indians, but perhaps by listening to their myths we will find some reason to rejoice with them.

First Myth
The Man Who Couldn't Be Told Anything[1]

This old man's family possessed just a small quantity of boiled pumpkins, when one day he asked to go find a few friends and invite them to eat these gourds. But instead, he called out to the people of all the houses in the village. He shouted as loudly as he could:

"Everyone come and eat! Everybody must come eat!"

1. This is the title given to me by the Indians.

"We're coming! Everyone is going to come!" the people answered. And yet there was scarcely one dish of pumpkins. So the first two or three to arrive ate up everything, and for those who kept showing up there was practically nothing left. Everyone was assembled in the old man's house and there was no longer anything at all to eat. "How can this be possible?" he said with amazement. "Why the devil did they ask me to invite the people to come eat? As for me, I did what I was told. I thought there was a heap of pumpkins. It's not my fault! It's always the others who make me tell lies! And afterwards they are angry with me because I was made to say what wasn't so!" Then his wife explained to him: "You have to speak softly! You need to say very softly, in a low voice:'Come eat some pumpkin!' " "But why did you tell me to invite the people who are here? I shouted so they could hear me!" The old woman grumbled: "What an old ignoramus that one is to invite all these people."

Some time later, he went around urging his kin to come harvest his watermelon patch. But once again everyone turned up even though there were only three stalks of watermelons. "We're going to gather my watermelon crop! There are a lot of them!" he had proclaimed in a very loud voice. And all the people were there with their sacks, standing over the three stalks of watermelons. "I really thought there were a lot of them," the old man said apologetically. "But there are pumpkins and *anda'i*[2]: take them!" The people filled their sacks with pumpkins and *anda'i* instead of watermelons.

After the harvest, the old man returned home. He met his granddaughter there: she was bringing him her sick baby to be treated by the old man, for he was a *tôoie'éh*, a shaman.

"Grandfather! Do something then for your great-grandson who has the fever. Spit!"

2. *Cucurbita moschata*.

"Yes, I will take care of him right away!"

And he commenced to spit on the little boy without stopping, completely covering him with saliva. The child's mother exclaimed:

"Not like that! You must blow! Blow too! Come now, take better care of him, old man!"

"Alright, alright! But why didn't you say that sooner? You asked me to spit on my great-grandson, but not to blow. So I did; I spat!"

Obeying his granddaughter, the old man then set to blowing on the child, blowing and blowing, without a pause. After a moment, the woman stopped him and reminded him that it was also necessary to search for the spirit of the sick one. The grandfather got up at once and began looking, lifting up the objects in all the nooks and crannies of the house.

"No, no, grandfather! Sit down! Blow! And you have to sing!"

"But why do you wait till now to tell me that? You asked me to look for my great-grandson so I got up in order to look for him!"

He sat back down and sent for the other sorcerers so they could assist him in his cure, help him to find again the spirit of his great-grandson. They all gathered together in his house, and the old man spoke to them thus:

"Our great-grandson is ill. Hence we shall try to discover the cause of his illness."

The old man had a she-ass as the domestic animal of his spirit. The spirits of the shamans undertook the journey. The old man climbed up on his she-ass and started his chant: "*Kuvo'uitaché! kuvo'uitaché! kuvo'uitaché!*... She-ass! she-ass! she ass!..." They walked in this way a fairly long while.

At a certain moment, the she-ass sank a hoof into the soft ground: there were pumpkin seeds there. The she-ass halted. The old man pointed out the fact to his companions: "The she-ass has just come to a halt. There must be something there!" They looked carefully and discovered a large amount of boiled pumpkins: they started eating them. When they were all done, the old man announced: "Well then! Now we can continue on our way."

They started off again, still keeping to the rhythm of the same chant: "*Kuvo'uitaché! kuvo'uitaché! kuvo'uitaché!*... she-ass! she-ass! she-ass! . . ." Suddenly the animal's ear cocked: "Aha!" said the old man. At that moment he remembered that near that very spot was a beehive that he had blocked up so that the bees would come back and make their honey there. The shamans cleared a path to allow the she-ass to reach that place. When they got near to the hive, they positioned the she-ass with its rump against the tree and, with her tail, she began extracting the honey. The old man said, "Suck the honey! Suck all the honey that's in the tail hairs! We're going to draw out some more." The beast repeated the operation and collected a lot more honey. "Go ahead, go ahead!" the old man said. "Eat all the honey, men with the same noses! Do you want more, or have you had your fill?" The other shamans were no longer hungry. "Very well then, let's move on!"

They set out once more, still chanting: "She-ass! she-ass! she-ass! . . ." They went on that way for a while. All at once, the old man cried out: "Aha! There's something up ahead! What can that be? That has to be a *ts'ich'e*, an evil spirit!" They came close to it and the old man declared: "Oh, that is a very swift being! We won't be able to catch up with it." And yet it was only a tortoise. "I'll stay in the middle and grab it," he said, "for I am older and more experienced than you." He arranged them in a circle and, at his signal, they all fell upon the tortoise: "She-ass! she-ass! she-ass! . . ." But the animal didn't make the slightest movement, for it was a tortoise. They got the better of it. The old man exclaimed, "How pretty it is! What a beautiful pattern! It will be my domestic animal. He picked it up and they got under way again, still chanting: "She-ass! . . ."

But before long, "Aha!" and they stopped. "The she-ass will go no further. Something is up ahead." They looked and spied a skunk. "He will be our dog!" the old man affirmed. "He is very pretty, a wild dog!" They encircled it and the old man himself took up a position at the center, declaring, "I am older and more skillful than you." And, to the chant "She-ass! she-ass! she ass! . . ." they went on the offensive. But the skunk disappeared into its burrow: "He went in there! I'll try to get him out." The old sorcerer stuck his hand through the opening, bent way down, and the skunk pissed in his face.[3] "Aiee!" he screamed. The stench was so great he nearly fainted. The other shamans scattered in confusion, crying: "That stinks! That stinks like hell!"

They took up their journey, all of them chanting in chorus, and soon they felt like having a smoke. The ear of the she-ass dipped and the animal halted once more."So now we will smoke a little," the old man decided. He was carrying all his smoking gear in a little sack; he started searching for his pipe and tobacco. "Ah, I didn't count on forgetting my pipe!" He searched everywhere, but without finding anything. "Don't budge!" he said to the others. "I'll go as fast as I can to get my pipe and tobacco." And he left, urging himself along with his chanting: "She-ass! she-ass! she-ass! . . ." At the end of the chant, he was already back with them.

"Here I am!"

"So you're back, are you? We'll smoke a little then."

They commenced to smoke.

When they were done smoking, they started out on their way again; they were still chanting. Suddenly the animal's ear pointed and the old man alerted his companions: "Aha! That sounds like dancing over yonder!" As a matter of fact, the beat of a drum could be heard. The shamans arrived at the place of merrymaking and began to dance. Each one of them joined up with a pair of danc-

3. In actual fact, the skunk projects a foul-smelling liquid contained in an anal gland.

ers. They danced for a while, then talked the women into going for a little stroll with them. They went out away from the dancing place, and all the shamans made love with the women. Their old chief copulated too. But he had hardly finished when he fainted, for he was very old.

"Houf! houf! houf!" His gasping grew heavier and heavier and finally, completely out of breath, he fell into a swoon. After a minute or two, he regained his senses: "Houf! houf! houf!" he went, heaving great sighs and becoming much calmer. He gradually recuperated, gathered his companions about him, and asked: "Well then? You too are satisfied?"

"Oh, yes! Now we are free! We can get going, and a lot lighter than before!"

And, intoning their chant, they got under way again. After a while, the trail became very narrow: "We'll clear this path so the she-ass won't stick thorns in her feet." It was full of cactuses. So they cleared the path and came to the spot where the trail widened again. They continued chanting: "She-ass! she-ass! she-ass! . . ." A motion of the animal's ear made them stop: "There is something up ahead! Let's go see what it is." They advanced and the old shaman saw that it was his helper spirits. He had already informed them of what he was looking for. He drew near them and they announced to him: "It is *Faiho'ai*, the spirit of charcoal, who holds the soul of your great-grandson. He has also enlisted the aid of *Op'etsukfai*, the spirit of the cactus."

"Yes, yes! Exactly! That's it! I know them very well, those spirits."

There were others, but those he did not know. Advised of all this by his helper spirits, he now knew where to find his great-grandson: in a storehouse.[4]

Perched on his she-ass, he went ahead chanting and arrived at

4. A hut made of branches, where the Indians store their provisions.

the place mentioned. But there he remained prisoner of the spiny branches of the structure. He took fright and called to the others for help. But seeing that they remained unconcerned, he gave out a howl. Only then did his shaman friends come to his aid, and thus he was able to retrieve the spirit of the sick boy. He brought it back home and re-inserted it in the body of the child. Thereupon, his granddaughter got up, took her cured child, and went away.

This old shaman had other granddaughters. They liked very much to go gather the fruit of the *algarrobo.* The next day at dawn they came looking for him.

"Our grandfather is already up?"

"Of course; I've been awake for a long time!"

"So! Let's go then!"

And he left to hunt for the black *algarrobo* with one of his granddaughters who was still single. He led her to a place that had a lot of trees and the young woman started gathering the fruit. As for him, he sat down to smoke. But already the desire came to him, little by little, to do something with his granddaughter, for the session the day before, with the women encountered during the journey, had aroused his passions. So he began to consider ways to seduce his granddaughter.

He collected a thorn from the *algarrobo* and stuck it in his foot. Then he pretended to be trying to pull it out. He groaned in a pitiful manner.

"Unh! Unh! Unh!"

"Oh! My poor grandfather! What on earth has happened to him?"

"An accident! I have a thorn in my foot. And it feels like it's going all the way to my heart!"

The young woman, upset, went over to him and the grandfather said to her – "Take off your belt, for bandaging my wound! Because I can't stand it any longer!" She did as he said, and the grandfather advised her to sit down: "Now then, raise your loincloth a little so

I can place my foot on your thighs. Unh! Unh! Aiee!" Awful moans! He was really hurting: "Let me put my foot on your thighs! Unh! Unh! How it hurts! I can't bear it any more! Spread your thighs a little bit. Aiee! Aiee!" And the sympathetic young woman obeyed. The old man was all excited, for she was now completely naked: "Hmm! What beautiful legs she has, my little granddaughter! Couldn't you move my foot a little higher, granddaughter?"

That's when he threw himself on her, exclaiming – "Aha! Now we are going to forget about your future husband!"

"Oh! Grandfather!" said the young woman, who didn't want to.

"I am not your grandfather!"

"Grandfather, I'll tell everything!"

"Well then, so will I! I'll tell everything too!"

He threw her down and thrust his penis into her. Once he was on top of her, he exclaimed: "Ho! You see! Now you are benefitting from my leftovers. The very last ones indeed!" Then they returned to the village. She was so ashamed that she didn't tell anything.

The old man had yet another granddaughter, and she was also unmarried. And he would have liked very much to take advantage of her as well. So he invited her to go with him to gather the fruit of the *algarrobo*, and, once there, he repeated the same charade with the thorn. But this time, he was more in a hurry; he showed his granddaughter the thorn and, without further ado, threw her on the ground and stretched out on top of her. He started to penetrate her, but the young woman gave a violent jerk and the old man's penis went and planted itself in a tuft of grass, jamming one blade of the grass inside, wounding him slightly: "Aiee! My granddaughter has stung my nose!"[5] Once again he threw himself on

5. According to the Chulupi social code, it would be coarse to call the penis by its name. Hence it is necessary to say: the nose.

top of her and they wrestled on the ground. At the right moment, the grandfather got it up, but he missed his target a second time, and, in his exertion, went and uprooted the whole tuft of grass with his penis. He started bleeding, covering the granddaughter's stomach with blood.

She made a big effort and managed to get out from under her grandfather. She caught him by the hair, dragged him to the cactus, and set about rubbing his face against the thorns. He pleaded, "Take pity on your grandfather!"

"I don't want to hear a word about my grandfather!"

"You are going to lose your grandfather!"

"That's all the same to me!"

And she continued thrusting his face into the cactus. Next she took him again by the hair and dragged him into the middle of a *caraguata* bush. The old man withstood this for a few moments, then attempted to get back up; but she prevented him from doing so. The *caraguata* thorns scratched his stomach, his testicles, and his penis: "My testicles! My testicles are being torn to shreds!" the grandfather protested. *Krr! Krr!* went the thorns, tearing open his skin. At last, the granddaughter left him sprawled out on the *caraguata* heap. The old man's head was already completely swelled up from all the needles stuck in it. The young woman collected her sack, returned home, and revealed to her grandmother what her grandfather had tried to do. As for the latter, who could barely see any longer because of the needles that covered his eyes, he groped his way back and dragged himself into his house.

There, his wife removed her loincloth and flailed away at his face with it. "Come here for a minute and touch what I have there!" she cried. And, taking his hand, she made him touch her *hlasu*, her vagina. She was in a rage.

"Yes! You like the things that belong to others; but you want nothing to do with what is yours!"

"I don't want any of your *hlasu*! It's too old! Nobody wants to use old things!"

Second Myth
The Adventures of the Jaguar

One morning the jaguar went out walking and came upon a chameleon. As everyone knows, the chameleon can go through fire without being burned. The jaguar exclaimed, "How I would like to play with the fire too!"

"You can play if you want, but you won't be able to bear the heat and you will burn yourself."

"Huh! Hmph. Why couldn't I bear it? I'm fast too, you know!"

"Well then! Let's go over there; the embers are not so hot."

They went there, but actually the embers burned brighter there than anywhere else. The chameleon explained to the jaguar how he had to go about it and passed through the fire once to demonstrate: nothing happened to him. "Good! Get out of the way! I'm going to go too. If you can do it, so can I!" The jaguar jumped into the fire and immediately burned himself: hsss! He managed to get through, but he was already half charred, and he died, reduced to ashes.

In the midst of all this, the *ts'a-ts'i* bird arrived and started crying: "Oh! My poor grandson! I'll never be able to get used to singing in the footsteps of a buck!" He came down from his tree; then, with his wing, he began gathering the jaguar's ashes into a pile. Next he poured water on the ashes and hopped over the pile: the jaguar got back up. "Whew, such heat!" he exclaimed. "Why the devil did I go to sleep out in the bright sun?" He set out walking again.

Before long, he heard someone singing: it was the buck, who was standing in the sweet potato patch. The sweet potatoes were really cactuses. "*At'ona'i! At'ona'i!* I am sleepy for no reason!" And as he sang, he danced over the cactuses: since bucks have very small feet, he could easily avoid the thorns. The jaguar watched his goings on.

"Ah! How I would like to dance there too!"

"I don't think you will be able to walk over the cactuses without getting spines stuck in your paws."

"And why not? If you can go through them, then I can go there just as well!"

"OK! In that case, let's go over there: there are fewer spines."

But there were actually a lot more. The buck went first to show the jaguar how it was done: he danced over the cactuses, then came back, without any spines. "Hee! Hee! Hee!" went the jaguar. "How much fun all that is!" It was his turn. He entered the cactus patch and at once the spines drove into his paws. Two leaps carried him to the middle of the cactus patch. He suffered great pain and could no longer keep himself standing: he lay down full length, his body riddled with spines.

The *ts'a-ts'i* appeared again, pulled the jaguar out of there, and removed all the spines one by one. Then, using his wing, he pushed him a little further. "Such heat!" exclaimed the jaguar. "Why the devil did I fall asleep in the hot sun?"

He set out again. A few minutes later, he met up with a lizard: lizards can climb up trees all the way to the ends of the branches and come back down very quickly without falling. The jaguar watched him do it and immediately felt like having fun too. So the lizard led him to another tree and showed him first how it had to be done: he went up to the top and came back down full speed. The jaguar dashed off in his turn, but on reaching the top of the tree, he fell and a branch rammed up his anus, coming out through his mouth. "Oh!" said the jaguar, "that feels just like when I have diarrhea." Again *ts'a-ts'i* came to get him out of the jam, nursed his anus, and the jaguar was able to start off once more.

He then encountered a bird who was playing with two branches that the wind was causing to cross one another. The bird was entertaining himself by going between them just as they crossed. The jaguar thought that looked like great fun. "Me too, I want to play too!"

"But you won't be able to do it! You're too big, not little like me."

"Who says I won't be able to?"

So the bird led the jaguar to another tree and passed through once to show him: the branches nearly touched the bird's tail when they came together. "Now it's your turn!" The jaguar sprang, but the branches caught him by the middle of his body, cutting him in two. "Aiee!" cried the jaguar. The two pieces fell and he died.

Ts'a-ts'i reappeared and saw his dead grandson. He started weeping: "I'll never be able to get used to singing in the footsteps of a buck!" He flew down and stitched the two pieces of the jaguar back together. With a snail's shell, he carefully smoothed out the seam; then he walked on the jaguar, who then got back up, alive.

He went on his way again. Then he saw *It'o* the royal vulture, who was amusing himself by flying up and down. That too delighted the jaguar: he announced to *It'o* that he wanted to play like he was doing. "Oh, my friend! How wonderful it would be to play like you!"

"That would be fine indeed, but you have no wings."

"That's true; I don't have any, but you can lend me some."

It'o agreed. He made two wings which he glued to the jaguar's body with some wax. When that was done, he invited his companion to fly. Together they rose to an incredible height and enjoyed themselves the whole morning long. But towards midday the sun was scorching hot and caused the wax to melt: the two wings came loose. The jaguar crashed to the ground with all his weight and died, practically smashed to bits. *Ts'a-ts'i* arrived, mended the jaguar's bones, and set him back on his feet. The jaguar started off again.

It wasn't long until he came upon the skunk, who was playing with his son, breaking pieces of wood. The jaguar came closer to see what was going on: he immediately pounced on the skunk's son, then tried attacking the father. But the latter pissed in his eyes and the jaguar was left blinded.[6] He walked and could no longer see a thing. But *ts'a-ts'i* appeared once more and gave his eyes a good washing; that is why the jaguar's vision is so good. Without the *ts'a-ts'i*, the jaguar would no longer exist.

The value of these two myths is not limited to the intensity of the laughter they produce. It is a matter of thoroughly understanding what it is about these stories that amuses the Indians; it also needs establishing that comic force is not the only property these two myths have in common. On the contrary, they constitute a set on the basis of less external reasons, reasons that enable one to see their being grouped as something other than an arbitrary juxtaposition.

The central character of the first myth is an old shaman. First we see him take everything literally, confuse the letter with the spirit (so that *he can't be told anything*), and, as a result cover himself with ridicule in the eyes of the Indians. Next we accompany him in the adventures his doctor's "trade" exposes him to. The zany expedition he undertakes with the other shamans, in search of his great-grandson's soul, is sprinkled with episodes that reveal the doctors' total incompetence and their prodigious capacity to forget the purpose of their mission: they hunt, they eat, they copulate, they seize upon the least pretext for forgetting they are doctors. Their old chief, after having brought about the cure just in time, gives free rein to a frantic debauchery: he takes unfair advan-

6. See note 3.

tage of the innocence and kindness of his own granddaughters so as to get under their skirts in the forest. In short, he is a grotesque hero, and one laughs at his expense.

The second myth tells us of the jaguar. Although it is a mere outing, his journey is not lacking in the unexpected. This big simpleton, who decidedly meets up with a lot of characters on his way, falls systematically into the traps laid for him by those he holds so haughtily in contempt. The jaguar is big, strong, and stupid; he never understands anything that happens to him, and without the interventions of an insignificant little bird, he would have succumbed a long time ago. Every one of his moves proves his doltishness and demonstrates the ridiculousness of the character. To sum up, these two myths present shamans and jaguars as the victims of their own stupidity and vanity, victims who, accordingly, do not deserve compassion, but rather hearty laughter.

This is the proper place to raise the question: who is being made fun of? The first conjunction shows the jaguar and the shaman brought together through the laughter their misadventures arouse. But when we examine the real status of these two types of beings, the Indians' real-life relationship to them, we find them placed side by side in a second analogy: the fact is, far from being comic figures, both of them are dangerous beings capable of inspiring fear, respect, and hatred, but never the desire to laugh.

In most South American Indian tribes, shamans share prestige and authority with the chiefs, that is, when they themselves do not fill that political function. The shaman is always a very important figure in Indian societies, and, as such, he is at the same time respected, admired, and feared. This is because in reality he is the only one in the group who possesses supernatural powers, the only one with the power to control the dangerous world of the spirits and the dead. Hence, the shaman is a man of knowledge who puts what he knows in the service of the group by caring for the sick.

But the same powers that make him a doctor, that is, a man capable of bringing life, enable him to rule over death as well. For that reason, he is dangerous, disquieting; one is constantly mistrustful of him. As the master of life and death, he is immediately made responsible for every extraordinary occurrence, and very often he is killed out of fear. This means, consequently, that the shaman moves within a space that is too distant from, too external to that of the group for the group to dream, in real life, of letting its laughter bring it nearer to him.

What of the jaguar? This feline is an effective hunter, for it is powerful and cunning. The prey it attacks most readily (wild hogs, animals of the deer family) are also the game generally preferred by the Indians. The result is that the jaguar is seen by them – and here the myths in which the jaguar appears supply a frequent confirmation of these facts based on observation – more as a competitor to be reckoned with than as a fearsome enemy. However, it would be a mistake to conclude that the jaguar is not dangerous. It is true no doubt that it rarely attacks men; but I know of several cases of Indians being attacked and devoured by this beast, so it is always risky business when one encounters the jaguar. Moreover, its very qualities as a hunter, together with the dominion it exercises over the forest, induce the Indians to accord it the full measure of respect and to refrain from underestimating it: they respect the jaguar as an equal and in no instance do they make light of it.[7] In real life, the jaguar and the laughter of men remain disjoined.

Let us conclude, then, the first phase of this summary investigation by stating that:

7. I have even noted among tribes having very different cultures, as, for example, the Guayaki, the Guarani, the Chulupi, a tendency to exaggerate the risk of meeting this animal: the Indians *play* at being afraid of the jaguar, because they really do fear it.

(1) The two myths considered present the shaman and the jaguar as grotesque beings and objects of laughter;

(2) As for the relations between men on one hand, shamans and jaguars on the other hand, insofar as these relations are actually experienced, the position of the shamans and jaguars is just the opposite of that presented by the myths: they are dangerous beings, hence worthy of respect, who by that very fact remain beyond laughter;

(3) The contradiction between the imaginary world of the myth and the real world of everyday life is resolved when one recognizes in the myths a derisive intent: *the Chulupi do in mythical life what is forbidden them in real life*. One does not laugh at real shamans or real jaguars, for they are not in the least bit amusing. For the Indians, it is a matter of challenging, of demystifying in their own eyes the fear and the respect that jaguars and shamans inspire in them. This calling into question can be carried out in two ways: in actual fact, in which case the shaman deemed too dangerous, or the jaguar encountered in the forest, is killed; or symbolically, *through laughter*, in which case the myth invents a variety of shamans and jaguars of a kind that can be ridiculed, stripped as they are of their real attributes and transformed into village idiots.

Let us consider the first myth, for example. The central part of it is devoted to the description of a shamanistic cure. The doctor's task is a serious matter, since, in order to heal the one who is sick, it is necessary to discover and re-integrate into the patient's body the soul held captive far away. This means that during the expedition undertaken by his spirit, the shaman has to give full attention to his work and cannot allow himself to be distracted by anything. Now what happens to him in the myth? First of all, there are many shamans, while the case to be treated is relatively mild: the child is running a fever. A shaman does not send for his colleagues except in really hopeless cases. Next, we see the doctors, like children, taking advantage of the slightest opportunity to play hookey: they eat (first boiled pumpkins, then the honey extracted by the she-ass's tail), they hunt (a tortoise, then a skunk); they dance with women (instead of dancing by themselves, as they should), and waste no time in seducing them, then going off to copulate with them (something a shaman at work must absolutely abstain from). During this time, the old man realizes he has forgotten the one thing a true shaman would never forget, that is, his tobacco. To top it off, he becomes entangled like a fool in a mass of thorns where his companions would leave him to thrash about if he did not howl for assistance. In short, the head shaman does exactly the contrary of what a genuine doctor would do. It is not possible, without overburdening the discussion, to recall all the traits that hold the mythical shaman up to ridicule. A brief word should be said about two of them, however: his "domestic animal" and his chant. Whenever a shaman of the Chaco undertakes a cure, he sends (in his imagination, of course) his pet animal out to explore. Every shaman is the master of such an animal helper spirit: more often than not, these are little birds or snakes, and in any case never animals as ludicrous (for Indians) as a she-ass. By choosing for the shaman a domestic animal so clumsy and stubborn, the myth indicates straight away that it is going to speak of a poor clown. Moreover, the songs of the Chulupi are always wordless. They consist of a slightly modulated chant, repeated indefinitely and punctuated, at infrequent intervals, by a single word: the name of the pet animal. Now the chant of our shaman is made up exclusively of his animal's name: in this manner, he is constantly issuing, like a victory cry, the confession of his shamanistic shenanigans.

Here we see emerge a cathartic function of the myth, so to speak: in its narration it frees one of the Indians' passions, the secret obsession to laugh at what one fears. It devalues on the plane of language a thing that cannot be taken lightly in reality, and, manifesting in laughter an equivalent of death, it instructs us that among the Indians, ridicule kills.

Although superficial thus far, our reading of the myths is nonetheless sufficient to establish that the mythological resemblance of the jaguar and the shaman is the transformation of a real resemblance. But the equivalence between them that we have brought to light remains external, and the characteristics that unite them always refer to a third term: the Indians' real attitude towards shamans and jaguars. Let us probe deeper into the text of the myths to see if the kinship of these two beings is not much closer than it appears.

It will be remarked first of all that the central part of the first myth and the second in its entirety speak of exactly the same thing. Involved in both instances is a *journey strewn with obstacles*: that of the shaman going off in search of the spirit of a sick boy, and that of the jaguar who is simply out for a walk. Now the quixotic or mock-heroic adventures of our two protagonists actually conceal, under the mask of a false innocence, a quite serious project, a very important sort of journey: *the journey that takes the shamans to the Sun*. Here we must invoke the ethnographic context.

The shamans of the Chaco are not merely doctors, but also soothsayers capable of seeing into the future (the outcome of a martial expedition, for example). Sometimes, when they do not feel certain of their knowledge, they go consult the Sun, who is an omniscient being. But the Sun, preferring not to be bothered, has placed a series of very difficult obstacles along the route leading to his abode. That is why only the best shamans, the most cunning and courageous, manage to stand the tests; then the Sun agrees to extinguish its rays and inform those who come before him. Expeditions of this kind, precisely because of their difficulty, are always collective and are always enacted under the direction of the most experienced of the sorcerers. Now, when one compares the ups and downs of a voyage to the Sun to the adventures of the old shaman, one notices that the two myths in question describe, often in precise detail, the stages of the Great Voyage of the shamans. The first myth tells of a cure: the doctor sends his spirit in search of the sick person's spirit. But the fact that the journey is conducted in a group already implies that more than a routine excursion is at stake, that something much more solemn is involved: a voyage to the Sun. Furthermore, certain obstacles encountered by the shamans in the myth correspond to the traps with which the Sun has marked out his road: the different barriers of thorns, for instance, and the episode with the skunk. The latter, by *blinding* the shaman, is repeating one of the moments of the voyage to the Sun: the passage through the darkness where one *does not see anything*.

In the end, what is found in this myth is a burlesque parody of the voyage to the Sun, a parody that takes its pretext from a theme that is more familiar to the Indians (the shamanistic cure) so as to poke fun at their sorcerers twice over. As for the second myth, it takes up, virtually element by element, the scenario of the voyage to the Sun, and the various games where the jaguar loses correspond to the obstacles that the true shaman is able to surmount: the dance in the thorns, the branches that criss-cross, the skunk that plunges the jaguar into darkness, and finally, the Icarian flight towards the sun in the company of the vulture. There is actually nothing surprising in the fact that the sun melts the wax that holds the jaguar's wings in place, since before the Sun will extinguish its rays the good shaman must have gotten over the previous obstacles.

Our two myths thus make use of the theme of the Great Voyage to caricature shamans and jaguars by showing them to be incapable of completing that voyage. It is not without reason that the indigenous mind chooses the activity most closely tied to the shaman's task, the meeting with the Sun; it tries to introduce a boundless space between the shaman and the jaguar of the myths and their goal, a space that is filled in by the comic. And the fall of the jaguar who loses his wings through recklessness is the metaphor of a demystification intended by the myth.

Hence we find that the two roads on which the shaman and the jaguar, respectively, are made to travel by the myths lead in the same direction; we see the resemblance the myths set out to elicit between the two protagonists gradually become more specific. But are these parallels destined to meet? An objection might be countered to the above observations: while it is perfectly consistent and, one might say predictable even, for the first myth to evoke the setting of the voyage to the Sun in order to make fun of those who accomplish the voyage – the shamans – one fails to understand, on the other hand, the conjunction of the jaguar qua jaguar and the theme of the Great Voyage; it is hard to comprehend why the indigenous mind calls upon this aspect of shamanism in order to deride the jaguar. Since the two myths examined do not throw any light on the question, it is again necessary to rely on the ethnography of the Chaco.

As we have seen, various tribes of this region share the conviction that good shamans are capable of reaching the abode of the Sun, which permits them both to demonstrate their talent and enrich their knowledge by questioning the omniscient heavenly body. But for these Indians there exists another test of the power (and malice) of the better sorcerers: the fact that the latter are able to *transform themselves into jaguars*. The points of similarity between these two myths now cease to be arbitrary, and the heretofore external relationship between jaguars and shamans gives place to an identity, since, from a certain viewpoint, *shamans are jaguars*. Our demonstration would be complete if the converse of this proposition could be established: are jaguars shamans?

Now another Chulupi myth (too lengthy to be transcribed here) provides us with the answer: in former times, jaguars were in fact shamans. They were bad shamans, moreover, for, instead of healing their patients, they sought rather to devour them. It would seem that the circle is now closed, since this last piece of information allows us to confirm what went before: *jaguars are shamans.* By the same token, another obscure aspect of the second myth becomes clear: if it makes the jaguar into the protagonist of adventures usually reserved for sorcerers, this is because it is not a matter of the jaguar as a jaguar, but the jaguar as a shaman.

The fact, then, that the shaman and the jaguar are in a sense interchangeable confers a certain homogeneity on our two myths and gives credibility to our initial hypothesis: namely, that they constitute a kind of group such that each of the two components of which it is composed can be understood only by reference to the other. Of course, we are now a long way from our point of departure. At the outset, the resemblance of the two myths was external; it was based solely on the necessity for the indigenous mind to bring about a mythical conjunction that was not possible in reality: that of laughter on one hand, the shaman and the jaguar on the other. The preceding commentary (and let me emphasize that it is by no means an analysis, but rather preliminary to such a treatment) attempted to establish that this conjunction concealed beneath its comic intent the identification of the two characters.

When the Indians listen to these stories, their only thought, naturally, is to laugh at them. But the comic element of the myths does not prevent their having a serious side as well. A pedagogical aim can be discerned in the laughter provoked: while the myths amuse those who hear them, at the same time they convey and transmit the culture of the tribe. They thus constitute the gay science of the Indians.

The Duty to Speak

To speak is above all to possess the power to speak. Or again, the exercise of power ensures the domination of speech: only the masters can speak. As for the subjects: they are bound to the silence of respect, reverence, or terror. Speech and power maintain relations such that the desire for one is fulfilled in the conquest of the other. Whether prince, despot, or commander-in-chief, the man of power is always not only the man who speaks, but the sole source of legitimate speech: an impoverished speech, a poor speech to be sure, but one rich in efficiency, for it goes by the name *command* and wants nothing save the *obedience* of the executant. Static extremes in themselves, power and speech owe their continued existence to one another; each is the substance of the other, and the persistence of their coupling, while it appears to transcend history, yet fuels the movement of history: there is a historical event when – once what keeps them separate, hence dooms them to nonexistence, has been done away with – power and speech are founded in the very act of their meeting. To take power is to win speech.

Of course, the above remarks refer first and foremost to societies based on the division: masters/slaves, lords/subjects, leaders/citizens, etc. The hallmark of this division, its privileged locus of proliferation, is the solid, irreducible, perhaps irreversible fact of a power detached from society as a whole since it is held by only a few members. It is power that, having become separate from society, is exercised over, and if need be, against society. The focus of attention here has been the whole series of societies with a State, from the most archaic despotisms to the most modern of totalitarian States, going by way of the democratic societies, whose State apparatus, for all its liberalism, nonetheless remains in remote control of *legitimate violence*.

Speech and power hand in hand, bosom friends even: nothing rings truer to our ears accustomed to that very message. Yet, the conclusive evidence of ethnology cannot be ignored: the savage world of tribes, the universe of primitive societies, or again – and it is the same thing – societies without a State afford our reflection, strangely, the same alliance of power and speech detected in societies with a State. Over the tribe reigns the chief, and the latter also reigns over the language of the tribe. In other words, and especially as regards the primitive American tribes, the Indians, the chief – the man of power – also holds the monopoly of speech. In the case of these Savages, the question to ask is not: who is your chief? but rather: who among you is the one who speaks? The master of words is what many groups call their chief.

It would seem then, that power and speech cannot be conceived of separately, since their clearly metahistorical bond is no less indissoluble in primitive societies than in formations with a State. It would be less than exacting, however, to stop at a structural definition of this relationship. In fact, the radical break that divides societies, whether real or possible, according to whether they have or do not have a State, is bound to affect the way power and speech are linked. How, then, does this bond operate in societies without a State? The example of the Indian tribes tells us.

A difference emerges in the combination of speech and power

that is both quite apparent and very profound. If in societies with a State speech is power's *right*, in societies without a State speech is power's *duty*. Or, to put it differently, Indian societies do not recognize the chief's right to speak because he is the chief: they require that the man destined to be chief prove his command over words. Speech is an imperative obligation for the chief. The tribe demands to hear him: a silent chief is no longer a chief.

Let there be no mistake; involved here is not the taste, so keen among many Savages, for fine speeches, oratorical talent, and facile language. Here it is not a question of esthetics, but of politics. The whole political philosophy of primitive society can be glimpsed in the obligation of the chief to be a man of speech. This is where the space occupied by power unfolds, a space that is not as one might imagine it. And it is the nature of this discourse whose repetition is scrupulously seen to by the tribe, it is the nature of this masterful speech that directs us to the real locus of power.

What does the chief say? What is the word of a chief like? First of all, it is a ritualized act. Almost without exception, the leader addresses the group daily, at daybreak and at dusk. Stretched out in his hammock or seated next to his fire, he delivers the expected discourse in a loud voice. And his voice certainly needs to be strong in order to make itself heard. As a matter of fact, there is no gathering around the chief when he speaks, no hush falls, everybody goes about their business as if nothing was happening. *The word of the chief is not spoken in order to be listened to.* A paradox: nobody pays attention to the discourse of the chief. Or rather, they feign a lack of attention. If the chief, by definition, must submit to the obligation to speak, the people he addresses, on the other hand, are obligated only to appear not to hear him.

In a sense, they lose nothing in the bargain. Why? Because the chief, for all his prolixity, literally says nothing. His discourse basically consists of a celebration, repeated many times, of the norms of traditional life: "Our ancestors got on well living as they lived. Let us follow their example and in this way we will lead a peaceful existence together." That is just about what the discourse of a chief boils down to. One understands why those for whom it is intended are not overly disturbed by it.

What does speaking signify in this instance? Why does the chief have to speak just in order to say nothing? To what demand, coming from primitive society, does this empty speech that emanates from the apparent seat of power respond? The discourse of the chief is empty precisely because it is not a discourse of power. In primitive societies, in societies without a State, power is not found on the side of the chief: it follows that his word cannot be the word of power, authority, or command. An order? Now there is something the chief would be unable to give; that is the kind of fullness his speech is denied. A chief forgetful of his duty who attempted such a thing as an order would be met by a sure refusal of obedience, and a denial of recognition would not be far behind. The chief crazy enough to dream not so much of the abuse of a power he does not possess, as of the use of power, *the chief who tries to act the chief*, is abandoned. Primitive society is the place where separate power is refused, because the society itself, and not the chief, is the real locus of power.

It is in the nature of primitive society to know that violence is the essence of power. Deeply rooted in that knowledge is the concern to constantly keep power apart from the institution of power, command apart from the chief. And it is the very domain of speech that ensures the separation and draws the dividing line. By compelling the chief to move about in the area of speech alone, that is, the opposite of violence, the tribe makes certain that all things will remain in their place, that the axis of power will turn back exclusively to the social body, and that no displacement of forces will come to upset the social order. The chief's obligation to speak, that steady flow of empty speech that he *owes* the tribe, is his infinite debt, the guarantee that prevents the man of speech from becoming a man of power.

Prophets in the Jungle

Indian America never ceases to frustrate those who try to decipher its great countenance. In view of the unexpected places where its truth sometimes resides, we are obliged to reconsider the placid image many have of it, bearing in mind that it may conform to this image as a ruse. Tradition has handed down to us a summary and superficially veracious geography of the South American continent and the people who inhabit it: on the one hand, the Andean Highland Cultures and all the glamour of their refinements; on the other, the cultures assigned to the Tropical Forest, a dark realm of tribes roaming through savannas and jungles. The ethnocentrism of this scheme is unmistakable; in a way familiar to the West, it opposes civilization to barbarism. To complement this arrangement, the more scholarly belief is expressed that the life of the mind achieves its nobler forms only when rooted in the presumably richer ground of a great civilization: the mind of Savages remains a savage mind.

Now there is a tribe that shows these notions to be untrue and proves the Indian world capable of surprising the Westerner who listens to a language which in former times would have found an echo: the Mbya Guarani. Because it flourishes in the pristine freshness of a world where gods and men are on familiar terms, the religious thought of these Indians takes on the density of a free and rigorous meditation. The Tupi-Guarani, of whom the Mbya are one of the last remaining tribes, present Americanist ethnology with the enigma of a peculiarity that drove them, starting prior to the Conquest, to search unceasingly for the hereafter promised by their myths, *ywy mara eÿ*, the Land Without Evil. The most spectacular consequence of this sacred quest, quite exceptional for South American Indians, is known to us: the great religious migrations spoken of in the accounts of the first chroniclers. Under the leadership of inspired shamans, the tribes marched off, and, through fasting and dancing, attempted to reach the fabulous abode of the gods in the east. But soon the frightful obstacle appeared, the painful limit, the great ocean, all the more terrible as it confirmed the Indians in their certainty that its other shore was where the eternal land began. That is why the undaunted hope persisted of reaching it some day, and the shamans, attributing their failure to a lack of fervor, patiently awaited the coming of a sign or message from on high to renew their attempt.

Hence the Tupi-Guarani shamans exerted a considerable influence on the tribes, especially the greatest among them, the *karai*, whose speech, complained the missionaries, contained all the power of the devil. Unfortunately, their writings do not give any indication regarding the content of the *karai* discourses: doubtless for the simple reason that the Jesuits were loath to make themselves the devil's accomplices by recording in their own hand the things the devil proposed to his Indian henchmen. But men such as Thevet, Nobrega, Anchieta, et al, unintentionally betrayed their censors' silence by acknowledging the seductive powers of the sorcerers' speech, which was, in their words, the main hindrance to the conversion of the Savages. At that point, the admission slipped in that Christianity confronted something in the spiritual domain of the Tupi-Guarani, that is, "primitive" men, which was so forcefully stated as to be a successful counter to the missionary endeavor. Surprised and bitter, the zealous Jesuits uncomprehendingly discovered, in the difficulty of their preaching, the finitude of their world and the inanity of its language: they observed in amazement that the diabolical superstitions of the Indians could be exalted to the highest regions of something that insisted on being called a religion.

Thus driven underground, all this ancient knowledge risked being lost forever if the last Guarani Indians, mindful of the danger to it and respectful of its memory, had not kept it alive. Although they were a powerful people in former times, only a small number of them survive in the forests of eastern Paraguay. Admirable for their perseverance in not renouncing themselves, the Mbya, whom four centuries of abuse could not humble, oddly persist in inhabiting their ancient land following the example of their ancestors, in faithful harmony with the norms decreed by the gods before leaving their dwelling place and entrusting it to men. The Mbya have managed to preserve their tribal identity against all the circumstances and trials of their past. In the seventeenth century, the Jesuits failed to convince them to forsake idolatry and rejoin the other Indians in the Missions. What the Mbya knew, and what strengthened them in their refusal, was the shame and the pain of seeing something they despised threaten their own substance, their point of honor, and their moral code: their gods and the discourse of their gods, gradually eradicated by the god of the newcomers. The originality of the Guarani lies in this refusal; that accounts for their very special place among the other Indians and is responsible for the interest they offer ethnology. In fact, one rarely sees an Indian culture continue to pursue its existence in conformity with the standards of its own system of beliefs, and succeed in keeping that particular realm relatively free of any borrowings. More often than not, contact between the white world and the Indian world results in an impoverishing syncretism where, under the mask of an always superficial Christianity, indigenous thought seeks only to postpone its own demise. But it so happens that the outcome was different in the case of the Mbya; for, to date, they have consistently doomed every missionary enterprise to failure.

This centuries-old resistance of the Guarani to the religion of the *juru'a*, the white men, thus carries the force of the Indians' conviction that their fate is bound up with the promise of the old gods: that by living on the evil earth, *ywy mba'e*, respecting the norms, they will receive from those on high the signs that will favor the opening of the road leading to the eternal land, beyond the terror of the sea. One might wonder at a phenomenon that could be represented as a kind of folly: namely, the constancy of that rigid assurance capable of traversing history without appearing to be affected by the fact. That would be to ignore the sociological impact of religious fervor. As a matter of fact, if the present-day Mbya still conceive of themselves as a tribe, that is, as a social unit aiming to preserve its distinctive features, it is essentially because this intention is projected against a religious backdrop: the Mbya are a tribe because they are a non-Christian minority, because the thing that cements their unity is their common faith. Hence the system of beliefs and values constitutes the group as such, and, conversely, the group's closing about itself induces it, as the jealous repository of a knowledge that is honored even on the lowliest plane of experience, to remain the faithful protector of its gods and the guardian of their law.

To be sure, the understanding of religious matters is unevenly distributed among the members of the tribe. The majority of the Indians are content, as is natural, to participate diligently in the ritual dances, respect the traditional norms of life, and gather to listen to the exhortations of their *pa'i*, their shamans. These latter are the time sages who, like the *karai* of old – filled with the same passions – abandon themselves to the exaltation of questioning their gods. Here one rediscovers the Indians' taste for the spoken word, both as orators and as listeners: masters of words and eager to utter them, the caciques-shamans always find in the rest of the Indians an audience ready to hear them.

These discourses almost always deal with the themes that literally obsess the Mbya: their lot on earth, the necessity to heed the norms laid down by the gods, their hopes of gaining the state of perfection, the state of *aguyje*, which alone allows those who reach it to see the road to the Land Without Evil opened to them by the inhabitants of heaven. The nature of the shamans' concerns, their meaning and import, and the manner in which the shamans reveal them, make it obvious that the word shaman is inadequate to describe the true personality of these men capable of verbal ecstasy when moved by the spirit of the gods. Sometimes healers, but not necessarily, they are much less concerned to restore health to the sick body than to acquire, through dance, that internal strength and firmness of spirit which alone are apt to please Ñamandu, Karai Ru Ete, and all the deities who figure in the Guarani pantheon. More than practitioners, then, the *pa'i* are meditators. Resting on the solid ground of myths and traditions, they devote themselves, each on his own account, to a veritable gloss on those texts. Hence, one finds among the Guarani what might be called two sedimentations of their oral "literature": one profane, that takes in the whole of their mythology, notably the great myth known as the myth of the twins; another sacred, that is, kept secret from the whites, and made up of prayers, religious songs, and, finally, all the improvisations wrung from the *pa'i* by their inflamed fervor when they feel a god desires to speak through them. These *pa'i*, whom one is tempted to call prophets instead of shamans, give the astonishing profundity of their discourse the form of a language remarkable for its poetic richness. We see in it a clear indication of the Indians' concern to delimit a sphere of the sacred so that the language which articulates it is itself a negation of secular language. Verbal invention, arising from the desire to name beings and things according to their hidden dimension, their divine essence, results in a linguistic transmutation of the everyday world, a noble style of speech sometimes mistaken for a secret language. In this way the Mbya speak of the "flower of the bow" to designate the arrow, the "skeleton of the fog" in naming the pipe, and "flowery branches" to evoke the fingers of Ñamandu. An admirable transfiguration which puts an end to the confusion and *ressentiment** of the world of appearances where the passion of the *last men* does not wish to be detained. What better name for the Mbya, Indians who are resolved not to outlive their gods?

The first light of dawn traces the tops of the great trees. There awakens simultaneously in the hearts of the Guarani Indians the anguish of their *tekoachy*, their troubled existence, once again brought into the light of the sun, calling them back to their fate as inhabitants of the earth. It is not uncommon at that hour to see a *pa'i* stand up. His voice is inspired by the invisible ones – it will be the locus of the dialogue between humans and the gods – and he bestows on the rigor of his Word the impetus of a faith that quickens the finer forms of knowledge. Savage matins in the forest, the solemn words of his lament are directed to the east, to their meeting with the sun, the visible messenger of Ñamandu, the mighty lord of those who live on high: this exemplary prayer is addressed to him.

Contradicting the first legitimate movement of hope, the words inspired in the supplicant by the rising sun gradually enclose him within the circle of distress where the silence of the gods has aban-

*The allusion here is to Nietzsche's notion of the hatred subjugated peoples feel for their masters, turned into a debilitating self-hatred or *ressentiment*. (Translator's note.)

doned him. The efforts of men to break free of their earthly condition appear futile since they do not move those whom they petition. But, having arrived at the furthest extreme of his doubt and anguish, the recollection of the past and the memory of ancestors returns to the one experiencing these feelings: in times past were not the dances, fasts, and prayers of the ancestors rewarded, and was it not granted them to cross the sea, to discover the way across? That means, then, that men have a claim to the attention of the gods, that everything is still possible. Confidence is thus asserted in a similar destiny for the men of the present, for the last *Jeguakava*: their waiting for the Words will not be in vain; the gods will make themselves heard by those who strain to hear them.

Such is the way the movement of entreaty is constructed; it comes at an early hour, and yet its hour is late. So Ñamandu, letting his light shine forth again, consents to let men live: their nocturnal sleep is a death from which the dawn rescues them. But for the *Jeguakava*, the wearers of the ritual masculine headdress, to live is not merely to awaken to the neutrality of things. The Mbya walk the earth as seekers, and the Father agrees to hear the complaint of his adorned ones. But as the hope arises on which the very possibility of questioning is based, the terrestrial weariness is working to slow its momentum. Flesh and blood are the measure of their fatigue, and prayer and dance can overcome it, especially dance, whose precise rhythm relieves the body of its earthly burden. What absence explains this quest so pressing that it ushers in the day? That of the *ne'e porä tenonde*, the primordial beatific words, the divine language where dwells the salvation of men. A pause on the threshold of their true abode: such is the life of the *Jeguakava* on the evil earth. Imperfection of body and soul prevents them from abandoning it. Imperfection is the only thing that keeps them this side of the frontier, the metaphorical sea, less frightening in its reality (which more often than not the Indians have not known) than for the fact that it is emblematic of the perhaps definitive allotment of the human and the divine, each rooted to its own shore. And yet, the desire of the Mbya is to please the gods, to merit the Words that will open the way to the eternal land, the Words that teach men the norms of their future existence. May the gods speak at last! May they recognize the effort of men, their fasts, their dances, their prayers! The *Jeguakava tenonde porängue'i*, the last of those who were the first to be adorned, no less rich in merits than their forefathers, long to leave the earth: then will their destiny be fulfilled.

What follows is an Indian's meditative prayer, tragic in the early morning silence of a forest: the clarity of its appeal is not marred by the underground presence of the Guarani feeling and taste for death, their destination; it is a token of their considerable wisdom that it is one road they know how to travel.

Father! Ñamandu! Again thou hast seen fit that I rise!
In like manner, again thou hast seen fit that the Jeguakava rise,
the adorned brothers in their totality.
And the Jachukava, the adorned sisters, again thou has seen fit that they too rise in their totality.
And as for all those thou hast not provided with the Jeguakava, thou hast seen fit that they too rise in their totality.
Hear me now: on behalf of the adorned ones, on behalf of those who are not thy adorned ones, on behalf of all of these, I question.

And yet, as for all that,
the words, thou dost not utter them, Karai Ru Ete:
neither for me, nor for thy sons bound for the indestructible land,
the eternal land which no pettiness alters.
Thou dost not utter the words where lie the future norms
of our strength, the future norms of our fervor.

For, in truth,
I exist in a manner imperfect,
my blood is of a nature imperfect,
my flesh is of a nature imperfect,
it is horrible, it is lacking in all excellence.
Things being thus arranged,
so that my blood of a nature imperfect,
so that my flesh of a nature imperfect,
shake themselves and cast their imperfection far from them:
with bended knees, I bow down,[1] *with a valorous heart in view.*
And yet hear this: thou dost not utter the words.

And so, because of all that,
it is surely not in vain that I myself am in need
of thy words:
those of the future norms of strength,
those of the future norms of a valorous heart,
those of the future norms of fervor.
Nothing now, among all things, inspires my heart with valor.
Nothing now points me to the future norms of my existence.

And the malefic sea, the malefic sea,
thou hast not seen fit that I myself cross it.
That is why, in truth, that is why, they are now
but few in number, my brothers,
they are now but few in number, my sisters.
Hear this: on behalf of the few who remain,
I make heard my lamentation.
On behalf of those, again I question:
for Ñamandu sees fit that they rise.

1. A description of one of the movements of the ritual dance.

Things being thus arranged,
as for those who rise, in their totality,
it is to their future nourishment they turn the attention
of their gaze, all of them;
and as the attention of their gaze is turned to their future
nourishment,
so they are those who exist, all of them.

Thou dost see fit that their words take wing,
thou dost inspire their questioning,
thou dost see fit that from all of them arises a great lamentation.

But hear this: I rise in my effort,
and yet thou dost not utter the words; no, in truth, thou
dost not utter the words.

Accordingly, this is what I am brought to say,
Karai Ru Ete, Karai Chy Ete:
those who were not few in number,
those intended for the indestructible land, the eternal land
which no pettiness alters,
all those, thou didst see fit that in truth they question,
in former times, concerning the future norms of their own existence.
And assuredly, they were given to know them in their perfection,
in former times.

And as for me, if my nature surrenders to its customary imperfection,
if the blood surrenders to its customary imperfection of times past:
then, assuredly, that does not come from all the evil things,
but from the fact that my blood of a nature imperfect, my flesh
of a nature imperfect are shaking themselves and casting their
imperfection far from them.

That is why, thou will utter the words in abundance,
the words whose soul is excellent,
for him whose face is not divided by any sign.[2] *Thou*
will utter them in abundance, the words,
oh! thou, Karai Ru Ete, and thou, Karai Chy Ete,
for all those intended for the indestructible land, the eternal
land which no pettiness alters,
Thou, You![3]

2. I.e., for those who refuse the Christian baptism.

3. This text was obtained in June 1966 in eastern Paraguay. It was recorded in the indigenous language and translated with the help of Léon Cadogan. I would like to take this opportunity to thank him.

Of the One Without the Many

It was after the flood. A sly and calculating god was instructing his son how to put the world back together: "This is what you will do, my son. Lay the future foundations of the imperfect earth ... Place a good hook as the future foundation of the earth ... the little wild pig will be the one to cause the imperfect earth to multiply ... When it has reached the size we want, I will let you know, my son ... I, Tupan, am the one who looks after the support of the earth ..." Tupan, master of the hail, rain, and winds, was bored; he was having to play by himself and felt the need for company. But not just anyone, not just anywhere. The gods like to choose their playmates. And this one wanted the new earth to be an imperfect earth, an evil earth, yet one capable of welcoming the little beings destined to stay there. That is why, seeing ahead, he knew in advance that he would have to face Ñande Ru Ete, the master of a fog that rises, heavy and dark, from the pipe he smokes, making the imperfect earth uninhabitable. "I sing more than Ñande Ru Ete. I will know what to do; I will return. I will make it so that the fog will lie light on the imperfect earth. It is only in this way that those little beings we are sending there will be cool, happy. Those we are sending to the earth, our little children, those bits of ourselves, will be happy. We have to fool them." The divine Tupan was mischievous.

Who is speaking thus in the name of the god? What fearless mortal dares, without trembling, to place himself on a level with one of the powers on high? He is not mad, however, this modest earth dweller. It is one of those little beings to whom Tupan at the dawn of time assigned the task of amusing him. It is a Guarani Indian. Rich in the knowledge of things, he is reflecting on the destiny of his people who choose to call themselves, with a proud and bitter assurance, the Last Men. The gods sometimes disclose their designs. And he, the *karai*, who is adept at understanding them and dedicated to speaking the truth, reveals what he learns to his comrades.

That particular night Tupan inspired him; his mouth was divine. He was himself the god and told of the genesis of the imperfect earth, *ymy mba'emegua*, the residence mischievously appointed for the happiness of the Guarani. He spoke at length, and the light of the flames illuminated metamorphoses: sometimes the calm face of the indifferent Tupan, and the sweep of the grand language; other times the anxious tenseness of an all too human face coming back amidst strange words. The discourse of the god was followed by the search for its meaning; the mind of a mortal sought to interpret its misleading evidence. The deities do not have to reflect. And the Last Men, for their part, are unresigned: they are the last no doubt, but they know why. And lo and behold, the inspired lips of the *karai* pierced the riddle of misfortune with an innocent commentary and a chilling revelation, whose brilliance is untainted by a trace of *ressentiment*: "Things in their totality are one; and for us who did not desire it to be so, they are evil."

Without question, this fragment lacks neither obscurity nor depth. The ideas expressed in it exert a double appeal: owing to their harshness, and their source. For these are the thoughts of a

Savage, an anonymous author, an old Guarani shaman deep in a Paraguayan forest. And there is no denying that they are not completely alien to us.

The question addressed is the genealogy of misfortune. The text points out that things are *evil*. Men inhabit an imperfect, evil earth. It has always been so. The Guarani are used to misfortune. It is neither new nor surprising to them. They knew about it long before the arrival of the Westerners, who taught them nothing on the subject. The Guarani were never good savages. They were a people relentlessly obsessed by the belief that they were not created for misfortune, and the certainty that one day they would reach *ywy mara-eÿ*, the Land Without Evil. And their sages, ceaselessly meditating on the means of reaching it, would reflect on the problem of their origin. How does it happen that we inhabit an imperfect earth? The grandeur of the question is matched by the heroism of the reply: Men are not to blame if existence is unjust. We need not beat our breasts because we exist in a state of imperfection.

What is at the root of the imperfection besetting men, *which we did not desire?* It arises from the fact that "things in their totality are one." A startling utterance, of a kind to send Western thought reeling back to its beginnings. Yet, this is indeed what Guarani thinkers say, what they are continually proclaiming – and they pursue its strictest consequences, its most unsettling implications: misfortune is engendered by the imperfection of the world, because all things that constitute the imperfect world are one. Being one is the property shared by the things of the world. The One is the name of the imperfect. To sum up the deadly concision of its discourse, Guarani thought says that the One is Evil itself.

The misfortune of human existence, the imperfection of the world, a unity seen as a rift inscribed at the heart of the things that comprise the world: that is what the Guarani reject; that is what has impelled them from time immemorial to search for another space where they might know the happiness of an existence healed of its essential wound – an existence unfolding towards a horizon free of the One. But what is this not-One so stubbornly desired by the Guarani? Is it the perfection of the world to be found in the Many, according to a dichotomy familiar to Western metaphysics? And do the Guarani, unlike the ancient Greeks, place the Good there where, spontaneously, we deny it? While it is true that one finds in the Guarani an *active revolt* against the tyranny of the One, and in the Greeks a *contemplative nostalgia* for the One, it is not the Many which the former embrace; the Guarani Indians do not discover the Good, the Perfect, in the mechanical disintegration of the One.

In what sense do the things said to be One fall by that very fact within the evil field of imperfection? One interpretation has to be ruled out, even though a literal reading of the fragment seems to invite it: that the One is the All. The Guarani sage declares that "things in their totality are One," but he does not name the All, a category perhaps absent from his thought. He explains that each of the "things," taken one by one, that make up the world – earth and sky, water and fire, animals and plants, and lastly men – is marked, graven with the seal of the One. What is a thing that is One? How do we recognize the mark of the One on things?

One is everything corruptible. The mode of existence of the One is the transitory, the fleeting, the ephemeral. Whatever is born, grows, and develops only in order to perish will be called the One. What does that mean? Here one gains access, via a bizarre use of the identity principle, to the foundation of the Guarani religious universe. Cast on the side of the corruptible, the One becomes the sign of the Finite. The world of men harbors nothing but imperfection, decay, and ugliness: the ugly land, the other name for the evil land. *Ywy mba'e megua*; it is the kingdom of death. It can be said – Guarani thought says – that everything in motion along a trajectory, every mortal thing, is one. The One: the anchorage of death. Death: the fate of what is one. Why are the things that make up the imperfect world mortal? Because they are finite; because they are *incomplete*. What is corruptible dies of unfulfillment; the One describes what is incomplete.

Perhaps we can see it more clearly now. The imperfect earth where "things in their totality are one" is the reign of the incomplete and the space of the finite; it is the field of strict application of the identity principle. For, to say that A = A, this is this, and a man is a man, is to simultaneously state that A is not not-A, this is not that, and men are not gods. To name the oneness in things, to name things according to their oneness, is tantamount to assigning them limits, finitude, incompleteness. It is the tragic discovery that this power (*pouvoir*) to designate the world and define its beings – this is this, and not another thing – is but an absurd apology for real power (*puissance*), the secret power that can silently declare that this is this *and, at the same time*, that; Guarani are men *and, at the same time*, gods. What makes the discovery tragic is that *we did not desire it to be so*, we others who know our language to be deceptive, we who never spared any effort in order to reach the home of the true language, the incorruptible dwelling place of the gods, the Land Without Evil, where nothing in existence can be called one.

In the land of the not-One, where misfortune is abolished, maize grows all by itself; the arrow brings the game back to those who no longer need to hunt; the regulated flux of marriages is unknown; men, eternally young, live forever. An inhabitant of the Land Without Evil cannot be named univocally: he is a man, of course, but also man's other, a god. Evil is the One. Good is not the many, it is the *dual*, both the one and its other, the *dual* that truthfully designates complete beings. *Ywy mara-eÿ*, the destination of the Last Men, shelters neither men nor gods: only equals, divine men, human gods, so that none of them can be named according to the One.

There is no people more religious than the Guarani Indians, who down through the centuries haughtily rejected servitude to the imperfect earth, a people of arrogant madness whose self-esteem was so great that they aspired to a place among the deities. Not so long ago they still wandered in search of their true native land, which they imagined, or rather knew, to be located over there, in the direction of the rising sun, "the direction of our face." And many times, having arrived on the beaches, at the edges of the evil world, almost in sight of their goal, they were halted by the same ruse of the gods, the same grief, the same failure: the obstacle to eternity, *la mer allée avec le soleil.**

Their numbers are small now, and they wonder if they are not living out the death of the gods, living their own death. *We are the last men*. And still they do not abdicate; the *karai*, the prophets, fast overcome their despondency. Whence comes the strength that keeps them from giving up? Could it be that they are blind? Insane? The explanation is that the heaviness of failure, the silence of the sky, the repetition of misfortune are never taken by them as final. Do not the gods sometimes deign to speak? Is there not always, somewhere deep in the forest, a Chosen One listening to their discourse? That night, Tupan renewed the age-old promise, speaking through the mouth of an Indian inhabited by the spirit of the god. "Those whom we send to the imperfect earth, my son, we will cause to prosper. They will find their future spouses; they will marry them and they will have children: *so that they might attain the words that issue from us*. If they do not attain them, nothing good will come to them. All that we are sure of."

That is why, indifferent to all the rest – all the things that are one – caring only to rid themselves of a misfortune they did not

*From Rimbaud's poem "Éternité." An approximation in English might be: "the sun become one with the sea." (Translator's note.)

desire, the Guarani Indians take comfort in hearing once more the voice of the god: "I, Tupan, give you these counsels. If one of these teachings stays in your ears, in your hearing, you will know my footsteps . . . Only in this manner will you reach the end that was foretold to you . . . I am going far away, far away, I say. You will not see me again. Therefore, do not lose my names."

Of Torture in Primitive Societies

1. *The law and writing*

No one is meant to forget the severity of the law. *Dura lex sed lex.* Various means have been devised, depending on the epoch and the society, for keeping the memory of that severity ever fresh. For us the simplest and most recent was the generalization of free and compulsory schooling. Once universal education became legislated fact, no one could, without lying – without transgressing – plead ignorance. For, in its severity, the law is at the same time writing. Writing is on the side of the law; the law lives in writing; and knowing the one means that unfamiliarity with the other is no longer possible. Hence all law is written; all writing is an index of law. This is one of the lessons to be drawn from the procession of history's great despots, all the kings, emperors, and pharaohs, all the Suns who were able to impose their Law on the peoples under them: everywhere and without exception, the reinvented writing directly bespeaks the power of the law, be it engraved in stone, painted on animal skins, or drawn on papyrus. Even the *quipu* of the Incas can be regarded as a type of writing. Far from being merely mnemotechnic instruments of accountancy, the knotted cords were primarily and of necessity a writing that asserted the legitimacy of the imperial law and the terror it was intended to inspire.

II. *Writing and the body*

Various literary works teach us how the law contrives to annex unforeseen places for its inscription. The officer of *In the Penal Colony*[1] explains in detail to the explorer the operation of *the machine for writing the law*:

> "Our sentence does not sound severe. Whatever commandment the prisoner has disobeyed is written upon his body by the Harrow. This prisoner, for instance" – the officer indicated the man –"will have written on his body: HONOR THY SUPERIORS!"

And, as if it were a matter of common sense, the officer replies to the explorer, who was astounded to learn that the condemned man did not know the sentence that had been passed on him: "There would be no point in telling him. He'll learn it on his body." And later:

> You have seen how difficult it is to decipher the script with one's eyes; but our man deciphers it with his wounds. To be sure, that is a hard task; he needs six hours to accomplish it.

Here Kafka designates the body as a writing surface, a surface suited for receiving the legible text of the law.

And if it is objected that something merely invented by a writer's imagination cannot be applied to the domain of social facts, the reply can be made that the Kafkian delirium seems in this case somewhat anticipatory, and that literary fiction prefigures the

1. Franz Kafka, "In the Penal Colony," in *The Complete Stories*, Willa and Edwin Muir, trans., New York, Schocken, 1971.

2. Martchenko, *Mon Témoignage*, François Oliver, trans., Paris, Éditions du Seuil (Coll. "Combats"), 1971.

most contemporary reality. The testimony of Martchenko[2] soberly illustrates the triple alliance, intuited by Kafka, between the law, writing, and the body:

> Et alors naissent les tatouages. J'ai connu deux anciens droits communs devenus des "politiques"; l'un répondait au surnom de Moussa, l'autre à celui de Mazaï. Ils avaient le front, les joues tatouées: "Communistes-Bourreaux," "Les communistes sucent le sang du people." Plus tard, je devais rencontrer beaucoup de déportés portant de semblables maximes gravées sur leurs visages. Le plus souvent, tout leur front portait en grosses lettres: "ESCLAVES DE KHROUTCHEV," "ESCLAVE DU P.C.U.S."
>
> [And then the tattoos appeared. I met two former common law prisoners who had become "politicals"; one answered to the nickname Moussa; the other was called Mazaï. Their foreheads and cheeks had been tatooed: "Communist-Butchers," "The communists suck the blood of the people." Later, I was to encounter many deportees who bore similar maxims engraved on their faces. Most frequently, their whole foreheads carried in big letters: "SLAVES OF KHRUSHCHEV," "SLAVE OF THE C.P.S.U."]

But there is something in the reality of the camps of the U.S.S.R. during the decade of the sixties that surpasses even the fiction of the penal colony. In the latter, the system of the law needs a machine for writing its text on the body of the prisoner, who passively submits to the ordeal. In the real camp, the triple alliance, carried to its extreme point of constriction, does away with even the necessity of a machine; or rather, *it is the prisoner himself who is transformed into a machine for writing the law*, and who inscribes it on his own body. In the penal colonies of Moldavia, the harshness of the law fixes upon the very hand, the very body of the delinquent victim for its declaration. The limit is reached; the prisoner is *utterly outlawed*: his body writes the decree.

III. *The body and the rite*

A very large number of primitive societies mark the importance they attach to the admission of their young people into adulthood by the institution of the so-called rites of passage. These initiation rituals often constitute a basic axis around which the whole social and religious life of the community is organized. Now the initiatory rite always involves a laying hold of the body. It is the body in its immediacy that the society appoints as the only space that lends to bearing the sign of a *time*, the trace of a *passage*, and the allotment of a destiny. What secret are initiates made privy to by the rite that, for a moment, takes full possession of their bodies? A recognition of the intimacy, the complicity of the body and the secret, the body and the truth revealed by the initiation, leads one to question further. Why must the individual body be the focal point of the tribal *ethos*? Why can the secret only be communicated by means of the social enactment of the rite on the *body* of the young people? The body mediates the acquisition of a knowledge; that knowledge is inscribed on the body. The significance of initiation is contained in the answer to the twofold question concerning the nature of the knowledge transmitted by the rite, and the function of the body in the performance of the rite.

IV. *The rite and torture*

> Oh! "*horrible visu – et mirabile dictu*." Thank God, it is over, that I have seen it, and am able to tell it to the world.

George Catlin[3] has just witnessed, for four days running, the great annual ceremony of the Mandan Indians. In the description he gives of it, as well as in the finely executed sketches that illustrate it, he cannot keep from expressing – despite the admiration he feels for these great warriors of the Plains – his horror and repugnance at seeing the ritual spectacle. An understandable response, considering that while the ceremonial is a taking possession of the body by society, the latter does not seize hold of it in just any manner: almost invariably – and this is what horrifies Catlin – the ritual subjects the body to *torture*:

> One at a time, one of the young fellows, already emaciated with fasting, and thirsting, and waking, for nearly four days and nights, advanced from the side of the lodge, and placed himself on his hands and feet, or otherwise, as best suited for the performance of the operation, where he submitted to the cruelties....

Holes pierced in the body, skewers forced through the wounds, hanging, amputation, "the last race,"* torn flesh: cruelty's resources seem inexhaustible.

And yet:

> The unflinching fortitude with which every one of them bore this part of the torture surpassed credulity; each one as the knife was passed through his flesh sustained an unchangeable countenance; and several of them, seeing me making sketches, beck-

3. G. Catlin, *Letters and Notes on the Manners, Customs, and Condition of the North American Indians*, New York, Dover, 1973.

*This refers to that part of the Mandan ordeal in which the already exhausted young men were made to run (or be dragged) until the weights attached to their arms and legs ripped the wooden pegs from their flesh, signaling the successful completion of the initiation. (Translator's note.)

> oned me to look at their faces, which I watched through all this horrid operation, without being able to detect anything but the pleasantest smiles as they looked me in the eye, while I could hear the knife rip through the flesh, and feel enough of it myself, to start involuntary and uncontrollable tears over my cheeks.

The explicitly declared techniques, means, and goals of the cruelty vary from tribe to tribe, and from region to region, but the object is always the same: the individual must be made to suffer. I myself have described elsewhere[4] the initiation of Guayaki young people, whose backs are furrowed over their entire surface. The pain always ends up being unbearable: keeping silent all the while, the individual being tortured loses consciousness. Among the celebrated Mbaya-Guaycuru of the Paraguayan Chaco, the young men old enough to be admitted into the warriors' ranks also had to go through the ordeal of suffering. With the aid of a sharpened jaguar bone, their penises and other parts of the body were pierced through. There too, silence was the price exacted by the initiation.

The examples could be multiplied endlessly and they would all tell us one and the same thing: in primitive societies, torture is the essence of the initiation ritual. But is not this cruelty inflicted on the body aimed solely at measuring the young people's capacity for physical resistance, at reassuring the society as to the quality of its members? Would not the purpose of torture in the rite be merely to furnish the occasion to demonstrate *individual worth*? Catlin expresses this classic viewpoint quite well:

> I have already given enough of these shocking and disgusting instances to convince the world of the established fact of the Indian's superior stoicism and power of endurance.... I am ready

4. Pierre Clastres, *Chronique des Indiens Guayaki*, Paris, Plon, 1972.

> to accord them in this particular, the palm.... My heart has sickened also with disgust for so abominable and ignorant a custom, and still I stand ready with all my heart, to excuse and forgive them for adhering so strictly to an ancient celebration....

If one lets it go at that, however, one is bound to mistake the *function* of the suffering, grant it far too little significance, and overlook its use by the tribe to teach the individual something.

V. *Torture and memory*

The initiators make certain that the intensity of the suffering is pushed to its highest point. Among the Guayaki, for instance, a bamboo knife would be more than sufficient to slice into the skin of the initiates. *But it would not be sufficiently painful.* Consequently, a stone must be used, with something of an edge, but not too sharp, a stone that tears instead of cutting. So a man with a practiced eye goes off to explore certain stream beds where these torturing stones are found.

George Catlin notes, among the Mandan, the same preoccupation with the intensity of suffering:

> An inch or more of the flesh on each shoulder, or each breast was taken up between the thumb and finger by the man who held the knife in his right hand; and the knife, which had been ground sharp on both edges, and then hacked and notched with the blade of another, to make it produce as much pain as possible....

And, like the Guayaki scarifier, the Mandan shaman shows not the least amount of compassion:

> When he is, by turning, gradually brought to this condition, there is a close scrutiny passed upon him among his tormen-

tors, who are checking and holding each other back as long as the least struggling or tremor can be discovered, lest he should be removed before he is (as they term it) "entirely dead."

Precisely insofar as the initiation is – undeniably – a test of personal courage, this courage is expressed (in a manner of speaking) by silence in the face of suffering. But after the initiation, when all the suffering is already *forgotten*, something remains, an irrevocable surplus, the *traces* left on the body by the wielding of the knife or stone, the scars of the wounds received. An initiated man is a marked man. The purpose of the initiation, in its torturing phase, is to mark the body: in the initiatory rite, *society imprints its mark on the body* of the young people. Now, a scar, a trace, a mark are ineffaceable. Inscribed in the deepest layer of the skin, they will always testify, as a perpetual witness, that while the pain may be no longer anything but a bad memory, it was nonetheless experienced in fear and trembling. The mark is a hindrance to forgetting; the body itself bears the memory traces imprinted on it; *the body is a memory*.

For, what is wanted is not to lose the memory of the secret imparted by the tribe, the memory of that knowledge henceforth held in trust by the young initiates. What does the young Guayaki hunter, the young Mandan warrior, now know? The mark is a sure sign of their membership in the group. "You are one of us, and you will not forget it." Martin Dobrizhofer[5] is at a loss for words to describe the rites of the Abipones, who cruelly tattoo the faces of the young women at the time of their first menstruation. And to one of them who cannot keep from groaning from the etching

5. M. Dobrizhofer, *Historia de los Abipones*, Universidad Nacional del Nordeste, Facultad de Humanidades, Resistencia (Chaco), 1967, 3 vols.

of the thorn needles, this is what the old woman who is torturing her shouts:

> Enough of your insolence! You are not dear to our race! Monster for whom a little tickling of the thorn becomes unbearable! Maybe you do not know that you are of the race of those who bear wounds and are counted among the victors? You appear softer than cotton. There is no doubt that you will die an old maid. Will one of our heros judge you worthy of uniting with him, frightened one?

And I recall how, one day in 1963, the Guayaki satisfied themselves as to the true "nationality" of a young Paraguayan woman: after pulling off her clothes, they discovered the tribal tattoos on her arms. The whites had captured her during her childhood.

Thus there are two obvious functions of initiation as the incription of marks on the body: measuring personal endurance, and giving notice of membership. But is this really all that the memory acquired in pain has to retain? Is it truly necessary for one to go through torture in order to always remember the value of the ego and maintain tribal, ethnic, or national consciousness? Where is the secret transmitted; where is the knowledge revealed?

VI. *Memory and the law*

The initiatory ritual is a pedagogy that passes from the group to the individual, from the tribe to the young people. An assertive pedagogy, and not a dialogue: hence the initiates must remain silent under the torture. Silence gives consent. To what do the young people consent? They consent to accept themselves for what they are from that time forward: full members of the community. *Nothing more, nothing less.* And they are irreversibly marked as such. This, then, is the secret that the group reveals to the young people in the initiation: "You are one of us. Each one of you is like us; each one of you is like the others. You are called by the same name, and you will not change your name. Each one of you occupies the same space and the same place among us: you will keep them. None of you is less than us; none of you is more than us. *And you will never be able to forget it.* You will not cease to remember the same marks that we have left on your bodies."

In other words, society *dictates its laws* to its members. It inscribes the text of the law on the surface of their bodies. No one is supposed to forget the law on which the social life of the tribe is based.

In the sixteenth century, the first choniclers described the Brazilian Indians as people without faith, king or law. To be sure, those tribes had no knowledge of the harsh, separate law, the law that imposes the power of the few on all others in a divided society. That is a law – the king's law, the law of the State – of which the Mandan and the Guaycuru, the Guayaki and the Abipones know nothing. The law they come to know in pain is the law of primitive society, which says to everyone: *You are worth no more than anyone else; you are worth no less than anyone else.* The law, inscribed on bodies, expresses primitive society's refusal to run the risk of division, the risk of a power separate from society itself, *a power that would escape its control.* Primitive law, cruelly taught, is a prohibition of inequality that each person will remember. Being the very substance of the group, primitive law becomes the substance of the individual, a personal willingness to fulfill the law. Let us listen once more to the words of George Catlin:

> But there was one poor fellow though, who was dragged around and around the circle, with the skull of an elk hanging to the flesh on one of his legs – several had jumped upon it, but to no effect, for the splint was under the sinew, which could not be

> broken. The dragging became every instant more and more furious, and the apprehensions for the poor fellow's life, apparent by the piteous howl which was set up for him by the multitude around; and at last the medicine man ran, with his medicine pipe in his hand, and held them in check, when the body was dropped, and left upon the ground, with the skull yet hanging to it. The boy, who was an extremely interesting and fine-looking youth, soon recovered his senses and his strength, looking deliberately at his torn and bleeding limbs; and also with the most pleasant smile of defiance, upon the misfortune which had now fallen to his peculiar lot, crawled through the crowd (instead of walking, which they are never again at liberty to do until the flesh is torn out, and the article left) to the prairie, and over which, for a distance of half a mile, to a sequestered spot, without any attendant, where he laid three days and three nights, yet longer, without food, and praying to the Great Spirit, until suppuration took place in the wound, and by the decaying of the flesh the weight was dropped, and the splint also, which he dare not extricate in another way. At the end of this, he crawled back to the village on his hands and knees, being too much emaciated to walk, and begged for something to eat, which was at once given to him, and he was soon restored to health.

What force propelled the young Mandan? Certainly not some masochistic impulse, but rather the desire to be faithful to the law, the will to be neither more nor less than the equal of the other initiates.

I began by saying that all law is written. Here we see a reconstitution, in a sense, of the triple alliance already discerned: the body, writing, and the law. The scars traced on the body are the inscribed text of primitive law; in that sense, they are *a writing on the body*. As the authors of *L'Anti-Oedipe* have so forcefully argued, primitive societies are first of all societes that *mark*. And to that extent, they are in fact societies without writing; but what this statement means primarily is that writing points to the existence of a separate, distant, despotic law of the State, such as Martchenko's fellow prisoners write on their bodies. And one cannot emphasize too strongly the fact that it is precisely in order to exorcise the possibility of that kind of law – the law that establishes and guarantees inequality – that primitive law functions as it does; it stands opposed to the law of the State. Archaic societies, societies of the mark, are societies without a State, *societies against the State*. The mark on the body, on all bodies alike, declares: *You will not have the desire for power; you will not have the desire for submission*. And that non-separate law can only have for its inscription a space that is not separate: that space is the body itself.

It is proof of their admirable depth of mind that the Savages knew all that *ahead of time*, and took care, at the cost of a terrible cruelty, to prevent the advent of a more terrifying cruelty: *the law written on the body is an unforgettable memory*.

Society Against the State

Primitive societies are societies without a State. This factual judgment, accurate in itself, actually hides an opinion, a value judgment that immediately throws doubt on the possibility of constituting political anthropology as a strict science. What the statement says, in fact, is that primitive societies are missing something – the State – that is essential to them, as it is to any other society: our own, for instance. Consequently, those societies are *incomplete*; they are not quite true societies – they are not *civilized* – their existence continues to suffer the painful experience of a *lack* – the lack of a State – which, try as they may, they will never make up. Whether clearly stated or not, that is what comes through in the explorers' chronicles and the work of researchers alike: society is inconceivable without the State; the State is the destiny of every society. One detects an ethnocentric bias in this approach; more often than not it is unconscious, and so the more firmly anchored. Its immediate, spontaneous reference, while perhaps not the best known, is in any case the most familiar. In effect, each one of us carries within himself, internalized like the believer's faith, the certitude that society exists for the State. How, then, can one conceive of the very existence of primitive societies if not as the rejects of universal history, anachronistic relics of a remote stage that everywhere else has been transcended? Here one recognizes ethnocentrism's other face, the complementary conviction that history is a one-way progression, that every society is condemned to enter into that history and pass through the stages which lead from savagery to civilization. "All civilized peoples were once savages," wrote Raynal. But the assertion of an obvious evolution cannot justify a doctrine which, arbitrarily tying the state of civilization to the civilization of the State, designates the latter as the necessary end result assigned to all societies. One may ask what has kept the last of the primitive peoples as they are.

In reality, the same old evolutionism remains intact beneath the modern formulations. More subtle when couched in the language of anthropology instead of philosophy, it is on a level with other categories which claim to be scientific. It has already been remarked that archaic societies are almost always classed negatively, under the heading of lack: societies without a State, societies without writing, societies without history. The classing of these societies on the economic plane appears to be of the same order: societies with a subsistence economy. If one means by this that primitive societies are unacquainted with a market economy to which surplus products flow, strictly speaking one says nothing. One is content to observe an additional lack and continues to use our own world as the reference point: those societies without a State, without writing, without history are also without a market. But – common sense may object – what good is a market when no surplus exists? Now, the notion of a subsistence economy conceals within it the implicit assumption that if primitive societies do not produce a surplus, this is because they are incapable of doing so, entirely absorbed as they are in producing the minimum necessary for survival, for subsistence. The time-tested and ever serviceable image of the destitution of the Savages. And, to explain that inability of primitive societies to tear themselves away from the stagnation of living hand to mouth, from perpetual alienation in the search for food, it is said they are technically under-equipped, technologically inferior.

What is the reality? If one understands by technics the set of procedures men acquire not to ensure the absolute mastery of nature (that obtains only for our world and its insane Cartesian project, whose ecological consequences are just beginning to be measured), but to ensure a mastery of the natural environment *suited and relative to their needs*, then there is no longer any reason whatever to impute a technical inferiority to primitive societies: they demonstrate an ability to satisfy their needs which is at least equal to that of which industrial and technological society is so proud. What this means is that every human group manages, perforce, to exercise the necessary minimum of domination over the environment it inhabits. Up to the present we know of no society that has occupied a natural space impossible to master, except for reasons of force or violence: either it disappears, or it changes territories. The astonishing thing about the Eskimo, or the Australians, is precisely the diversity, imagination, and fine quality of their technical activity, the power of invention and efficiency evident in the tools used by those peoples. Furthermore, one only has to spend a little time in an ethnographic museum: the quality of workmanship displayed in manufacturing the implements of everyday life makes nearly every humble tool into a work of art. Hence there is no hierarchy in the technical domain; there is no superior or inferior technology. The only measure of how well a society is equipped in technology is its ability to meet its needs in a given environment. And from this point of view, it does not appear in the least that primitive societies prove incapable of providing themselves with the means to achieve that end. Of course, the power of technical innovation shown by primitive societies spreads over a period of time. Nothing is immediately given; there is always the patient work of observation and research, the long succession of trials and errors, successes and failures. Prehistorians inform us of the number of millenia required by the men of the Paleolithic to replace the crude bifaces of the beginning with the admirable blades of the Solutrian. From another viewpoint, one notes that the discovery of agriculture and the domestication of plants occurred at about the same time in America and the Old World. One is forced to acknowledge that the Amerindians are in no way inferior – quite the contrary – in the art of selecting and differentiating between manifold varieties of useful plants.

Let us dwell a moment on the disastrous interest that induced the Indians to want metal implements. This bears directly on the question of the economy in primitive societies, but not in the way one might think. It is contended that these societies are doomed to a subsistence economy because of their technological inferiority. As we have just seen, that argument has no basis either in logic or in fact. *Not in logic*, because there is no abstract standard in terms of which technological "intensities" can be measured: the technical apparatus of one society is not *directly* comparable to that of another society, and there is no justification for contrasting the rifle with the bow. *Nor in fact*, seeing that archaeology, ethnography, botany, etc. give us clear proof of the efficiency and economy of performance of the primitive technologies. Hence, if primitive societies are based on a subsistence economy, it is not for want of technological know-how. This is in fact the true question: is the economy of these societies really a subsistence economy? If one gives a meaning to words, if by subsistence economy one is not content to understand an economy without a market and without a surplus – which would be a simple truism, the assertion of a difference – then one is actually affirming that this type of economy permits the society it sustains to merely subsist; one is affirming that this society continually calls upon the totality of its productive forces to supply its members with the minimum necessary for subsistence.

There is a stubborn prejudice in that notion, one which oddly enough goes hand in hand with the contradictory and no less common idea that the Savage is lazy. While, in our culture's vulgar language, there is the saying "to work like a nigger," there is a similar expression in South America, where one says "lazy like an Indian." Now, one cannot have it both ways: either man in primitive societies (American and others) lives in a subsistence economy and spends most of his time in the search for food; or else he does not live in a subsistence economy and can allow himself prolonged hours of leisure, smoking in his hammock. That is what made an unambiguously unfavorable impression on the first European observers of the Indians of Brazil. Great was their disapproval on seeing that those strapping men glowing with health preferred to deck themselves out like women with paint and feathers instead of perspiring away in their gardens. Obviously, these people were deliberately ignorant of the fact that one must earn his daily bread by the sweat of his brow. It wouldn't do, and it didn't last: the Indians were soon put to work, and they died of it. As a matter of fact, two axioms seem to have guided the advance of Western civilization from the outset: the first maintains that true societies unfold in the protective shadow of the State; the second states a categorical imperative: man must work.

The Indians devoted relatively little time to what is called work. And even so, they did not die of hunger. The chronicles of the period are unanimous in describing the fine appearance of the adults, the good health of the many children, the abundance and variety of things to eat. Consequently, the subsistence economy in effect among the Indian tribes did not by any means imply an anxious, full-time search for food. It follows that a subsistence economy is compatible with a substantial limitation of the time given to productive activities. Take the case of the South American tribes who practiced agriculture, the Tupi-Guarani, for example, whose idleness was such a source of irritation to the French and the Portuguese. The economic life of those Indians was primarily based on agriculture, secondarily on hunting, fishing, and gathering. The same garden plot was used for from four to six consecutive years, after which it was abandoned, owing either to the depletion of the soil, or, more likely, to an invasion of the cultivated space by a parasitic vegetation that was difficult to eliminate. The biggest part of the work, performed by the men, consisted of clearing the necessary area by the slash and burn technique, using stone axes. This job, accomplished at the end of the rainy season, would keep the men busy for a month or two. Nearly all the rest of the agricultural process – planting, weeding, harvesting – was the responsibility of the women, in keeping with the sexual division of labor. This happy conclusion follows: the men (i.e., one-half the population) worked about two months every four years! As for the rest of the time, they reserved it for occupations experienced not as pain but as pleasure: hunting and fishing; entertainments and drinking sessions; and finally for satisfying their passionate liking for warfare.

Now, these qualitative and impressionistic pieces of information find a striking confirmation in recent research – some of it still in progress – of a rigorously conclusive nature, since it involves measuring the time spent working in societies with a subsistence economy. The figures obtained, whether they concern nomad hunters of the Kalahari Desert, or Amerindian sedentary agriculturists, reveal a mean apportionment of less than four hours daily for ordinary work time. J. Lizot, who has been living for several years among the Yanomami Indians of the Venezuelan Amazon region, has chronometrically established that the average length of time spent working each day by adults, *including all activities*, barely exceeds three hours. Although I did not carry out similar measurements among the Guayaki, who are nomad hunters of the Paraguayan forest, I can affirm that those Indians, women and men, spent at least half the day in almost total idleness since hunting and collecting took place (but not every day) between six and eleven o'clock in the morning, or thereabouts. It is probable that similar studies conducted among the remaining primitive peoples would produce analogous results, taking ecological differences into account.

Thus we find ourselves at a far remove from the wretchedness that surrounds the idea of subsistence economy. Not only is man in primitive societies not bound to the animal existence that would derive from a continual search for the means of survival, but this result is even bought at the price of a remarkably short period of activity. This means that primitive societies have at their disposal, if they so desire, all the time necessary to increase the production of material goods. Common sense asks then: why would the men living in those societies want to work and produce more, given that three or four hours of peaceful activity suffice to meet the needs of the group? What good would it do them? What purpose would be served by the surplus thus accumulated? What would it be used for? Men work more than their needs require only when forced to. And it is just that kind of force which is absent from the primitive world; the absence of that external force even defines the nature of primitive society. The term, subsistence economy, is acceptable for describing the economic organization of those societies, provided it is taken to mean *not* the necessity that derives from a *lack*, an incapacity inherent in that type of society and its technology; but the contrary: the refusal of a useless *excess*, the determination to make productive activity agree with the satisfaction of needs. And nothing more. Moreover, a closer look at things will show there is actually the production of a surplus in primitive societies: the quantity of cultivated plants produced (manioc, maize, tobacco, and so on) always exceeds what is necessary for the group's consumption, it being understood that this production over and above is included in the usual time spent working. That surplus, obtained without surplus labor, is consumed, consummated, for political purposes properly so called, on festive occasions, when invitations are extended, during visits by outsiders, and so forth.

The advantage of a metal ax over a stone ax is too obvious to require much discussion: one can do perhaps ten times as much work with the first in the same amount of time as with the second; or else, complete the same amount of work in one-tenth the time. And when the Indians discovered the productive superiority of the white men's axes, they wanted them not in order to produce more in the same amount of time, but to produce as much in a period of time ten times shorter. Exactly the opposite occurred, for, with the metal axes, the violence, the force, the power which the civilized newcomers brought to bear on the Savages created havoc in the primitive Indian world.

Primitive societies are, as Lizot writes with regard to the Yanomami, societies characterized by the rejection of work: "The Yanomamis' contempt for work and their disinterest in technological progress per se are beyond question."[1] The first leisure societies, the first affluent societies, according to M. Sahlin's apt and playful expression.

If the project of establishing an economic anthropology of primitive societies as an independent discipline is to have any meaning, the latter cannot derive merely from a scrutiny of the economic life of those societies: one would remain within the confines of

1. J. Lizot, "Économie ou société? Quelques thèmes à propos de l'étude d'une communauté d'Amérindiens," *Journal de la Société des Américanistes*, vol. 9, (1973), pp. 137–75.

an ethnology of description, the description of a *non-autonomous* dimension of primitive social life. Rather, it is when that dimension of the "total social fact" is constituted as an autonomous sphere that the notion of an economic anthropology appears justified: when the refusal of work disappears, when the taste for accumulation replaces the sense of leisure; in a word, when the external force mentioned above makes its appearance in the social body. That force without which the Savages would never surrender their leisure, that force which destroys society insofar as it is primitive society, is the power to compel; it is the power of coercion; it is political power. But economic anthropology is invalidated in any case; in a sense, it loses its object at the very moment it thinks it has grasped it: *the economy becomes a political economy*.

For man in primitive societies, the activity of production is measured precisely, delimited by the needs to be satisfied, it being understood that what is essentially involved is energy needs: production is restricted to replenishing the stock of energy expended. In other words, it is life as nature that – excepting the production of goods socially consumed on festive occasions – establishes and determines the quantity of time devoted to reproduction. This means that once its needs are fully satisfied nothing could induce primitive society to produce more, that is, to alienate its time by working for no good reason when that time is available for idleness, play, warfare, or festivities. What are the conditions under which this relationship between primitive man and the activity of production can change? Under what conditions can that activity be assigned a goal other than the satisfaction of energy needs? This amounts to raising the question of the origin of work as alienated labor.

In primitive society – an essentially egalitarian society – men control their activity, control the circulation of the products of that activity: they act only on their own behalf, even though the law of exchange mediates the direct relation of man to his product. Everything is thrown into confusion, therefore, when the activity of production is diverted from its initial goal, when, instead of producing only for himself, primitive man also produces for others, *without exchange and without reciprocity*. That is the point at which it becomes possible to speak of labor: when the egalitarian rule of exchange ceases to constitute the "civil code" of the society, when the activity of production is aimed at satisfying the needs of others, when the order of exchange gives way to the terror of debt. It is there, in fact, that the difference between the Amazonian Savage and the Indian of the Inca empire is to be placed. All things considered, the first produces in order to live, whereas the second works in addition so that others can live, those who do not work, the masters who tell him: you must pay what you owe us, you must perpetually repay your debt to us.

When, in primitive society, the economic dynamic lends itself to definition as a distinct and autonomous domain, when the activity of production becomes alienated, accountable labor, levied by men who will enjoy the fruits of that labor, what has come to pass is that society has been divided into rulers and ruled, masters and subjects – it has ceased to exorcise the thing that will be its ruin: power and the respect for power. Society's major division, the division that is the basis for all the others, including no doubt the division of labor, is the new vertical ordering of things between a base and a summit; it is the great political cleavage between those who hold the force, be it military or religious, and those subject to that force. The political relation of power precedes and founds the economic relation of exploitation. Alienation is political before it is economic; power precedes labor; the economic derives from the political; the emergence of the State determines the advent of classes.

Incompletion, unfulfillment, lack: the nature of primitive societies is not to be sought in that direction. Rather, it asserts itself as positivity, as a mastery of the natural milieu and the social project; as the sovereign will to let nothing slip outside its being that might alter, corrupt, and destroy it. This is what needs to be firmly grasped: primitive societies are not overdue embryos of subsequent societies, social bodies whose "normal" development was arrested by some strange malady; they are not situated at the commencement of a historical logic leading straight to an end given ahead of time, but recognized only a posteriori as our own social system. (If history is that logic, how is it that primitive societies still exist?) All the foregoing is expressed, at the level of economic life, by the refusal of primitive societies to allow work and production to engulf them; by the decision to restrict supplies to socio-political needs; by the intrinsic impossibility of competition (in a primitive society what would be the use of being a rich man in the midst of poor men?); in short, by the prohibition – unstated but said nonetheless – of inequality.

Why is the economy in a primitive society not a political economy? This is due to the evident fact that in primitive societies the economy is not autonomous. It might be said that in this sense primitive societies are societies without an economy, *because they refuse an economy*. But, in that case, must one again define the political in these societies in terms of an absence? Must it be suppposed that, since we are dealing with "lawless and kingless" societies, they lack a field of political activity? And would we not, in that way, fall into the classic rut of an ethnocentrism for which "lack" is the salient feature at all levels of societies that are different?

Let us discuss, then, the question of the political dimension in primitive societies. It is not simply a matter of an "interesting" problem, a subject to be pondered by specialists alone. For, in this instance, ethnology would have to be broad enough in scope to meet the requirements of a general theory (yet to be constructed) of society and history. The extraordinary diversity of types of social organization, the profusion, in time and space, of dissimilar societies, do not, however, prevent the possibility of discovering an order within the discontinuous, the possibility of a reduction of that infinite multiplicity of differences. A massive reduction, seeing that history affords us in fact only *two* types of society utterly irreducible to one another, two macro-classes, each one of which encompasses societies that have something basic in common, notwithstanding their differences. *On the one hand, there are primitive societies, or societies without a State; on the other hand, there are societies with a State.* It is the presence or absence of the State apparatus (capable of assuming many forms) that assigns every society its logical place, and lays down an irreversible line of discontinuity between the two types of society. The emergence of the State brought about the great typological division between Savage and Civilized man; it created the unbridgeable gulf whereby everything was changed, for, on the other side, Time became History. It has often been remarked, and rightly so, that the movement of world history was radically affected by two accelerations in its rhythm. The impetus of the first was furnished by what is termed the Neolithic Revolution (the domestication of animals, agriculture, the discovery of the arts of weaving and pottery, the subsequent sedentarization of human groups, and so forth). We are still living, and increasingly so, if one may put it that way, within the prolongation of the second acceleration, the Industrial Revolution of the nineteenth century.

Obviously, there is no doubt that the Neolithic break drastically altered the conditions of material existence of the formerly Paleolithic peoples. But was that transformation profound enough to have affected the very being of the societies concerned? Is it possible to say that societies function differently according to whether they are pre-Neolithic or post-Neolithic? There is ethnographic evidence that points, rather, to the contrary. The transition from nomadism to sedentarization is held to be the most significant consequence of the Neolithic Revolution, in that it made possible – through the concentration of a stabilized population – cities and, beyond that, the formation of state machines. But that hypothesis carries with it the assumption that every technological "complex" without agriculture is of necessity consigned to nomadism. The inference is ethnographically incorrect: an economy of hunting, fishing, and gathering does not necessarily demand a nomadic way of life. There are several examples, in America and elsewhere, attesting that the absence of agriculture is compatible with sedentariness. This justifies the assumption that if some peoples did not acquire agriculture even though it was ecologically feasible, it was not because they were incompetent, technologically backward, or culturally inferior, but, more simply, because they had no need of it.

The post-Columbian history of America offers cases of populations comprised of sedentary agriculturists who, experiencing the effects of a technical revolution (the acquisition of the horse and, secondarily, firearms) elected to abandon agriculture and devote themselves almost exclusively to hunting, whose yield was multiplied by the tenfold increase in mobility that came from using the horse. Once they were mounted, the tribes of the Plains of North America and those of the Chaco intensified and extended their movements; but their nomadism bore little resemblance to the descriptions generally given of bands of hunters and gatherers such as the Guayaki of Paraguay, and their abandonment of agriculture did not result in either a demographic scattering or a transformation of their previous social organization.

What is to be learned from the movement of the greatest number of societies from hunting to agriculture, and the reverse movement, of a few others, from agriculture to hunting? It appears to have been affected without changing the nature of those societies in any way. It would appear that where their conditions of material existence were all that changed, they remained as they were; that the Neolithic Revolution – while it did have a considerable effect on the material life of the human groups then existing, doubtless making life easier for them – did not mechanically bring about an overturning of the social order. In other words, as regards primitive societies, a transformation at the level of what Marxists term the economic infrastructure is not necessarily "reflected" in its corollary, the political superstructure, since the latter appears to be independent of its material base. The American continent clearly illustrates the independence of the economy and society with respect to one another. Some groups of hunters-fishers-gatherers, be they nomads or not, present the same socio-political characteristics as their sedentary agriculturist neighbors: different "infrastructures," the same "superstructure." Conversely, the meso-American societies – imperial societies, societies with a State – depended on an agriculture that, although more intensive than elsewhere, nevertheless was very similar, from the standpoint of its technical level, to the agriculture of the "savage" tribes of the Tropical Forest; the same "infrastructure," different "superstructures," since in the one case it was a matter of societies without a State, in the other case full-fledged States.

Hence, it is the Political break [*coupure*] that is decisive, and not the economic transformation. The true revolution in man's protohistory is not the Neolithic, since it may very well leave the previously existing social organization intact; it is the political revolution, that mysterious emergence – irreversible, fatal to primitive societies – of the thing we know by the name of the State. And if one wants to preserve the Marxist concepts of infrastructure and superstructure, then perhaps one must acknowledge that the infrastructure is the political, and the superstructure is the economic. Only one structural, cataclysmic upheaval is capable of transforming primitive society, destroying it in the process: the mutation that causes to rise up within that society, or from outside it, the thing whose very absence defines primitive society, hierarchical authority, the power relation, the subjugation of men – in a word, the State. It would be quite futile to search for the cause of the event in a hypothetical modification of the relations of production in primitive society, a modification that, dividing society gradually into rich and poor, exploiters and exploited, would mechanically lead to the establishment of an organ enabling the former to exercise power over the latter; leading, that is, to the birth of the State.

Not only is such a modification of the economic base hypothetical, it is also impossible. For the system of production of a given society to change in the direction of an intensification of work with a view to producing a greater quantity of goods, either the men living in that society must desire the transformation of their mode of life, or else, not desiring it, they must have it imposed on them by external violence. In the second instance, nothing originates in the society itself; it suffers the aggression of an external power for whose benefit the productive system will be modified: more work and more production to satisfy the needs of the new masters of power. Political oppression determines, begets, allows exploitation. But it serves no purpose to evoke such a "scenario," since it posits an external, contingent, immediate origin of State violence, and not the slow fruition of the internal, socioeconomic conditions of its rise.

It is said that the State is the instrument that allows the ruling class to bring its violent domination to bear on the dominated classes. Let us assume that to be true. For the State to appear, then, there would have to exist a prior division of societies into antagonistic social classes, tied to one another by relations of exploitation. Hence the *structure* of society – the division into classes –

would have to precede the emergence of the State *machine*. Let me point out, in passing, the extreme fragility of that purely instrumentalist theory of the State. If society is organized by oppressors who are able to exploit the oppressed, this is because that ability to impose alienation rests on the use of a certain force, that is, on the thing that constitutes the very substance of the State, "the monopoly of legitimate physical violence." That being granted, what necessity would be met by the existence of a State, since its essence – violence – is inherent in the division of society, and, in that sense, it is already given in the oppression that one group inflicts on the others? It would be no more than the useless organ of a function that is filled beforehand and elsewhere.

Tying the emergence of the State machine to a transformation of the social structure results merely in deferring the problem of that emergence. For then one must ask why the new division of men into rulers and ruled within a primitive society, that is, an undivided society, occurred. What motive force was behind that transformation that culminated in the formation of the State? One might reply that its emergence gave legal sanction to a private property that had come into existence previously. Very good. But why would private property spring up in a type of society in which it is unknown because it is rejected? Why would a few members want to proclaim one day: *this is mine*, and how could the others allow the seeds of the thing primitive society knows nothing about – authority, oppression, the State – to take hold? The knowledge of primitive societies that we now have no longer permits us to look for the origin of the political at the level of the economic. That is not the soil in which the genealogy of the State has its roots. There is nothing in the economic working of a primitive society, a society without a State, that enables a difference to be introduced making some richer or poorer than others, because no one in such a society feels the quaint desire to do more, own more, or appear to be more than his neighbor. The ability, held by all cultures alike, to satisfy their material needs, and the exchange of goods and services, which continually prevents the private accumulation of goods, quite simply make it impossible for such a desire – the desire for possession that is actually the desire for power – to develop. Primitive society, the first society of abundance, leaves no room for the desire for overabundance.

Primitive societies are societies without a State because for them the State is impossible. And yet all civilized peoples were first primitives: what made it so that the State ceased to be impossible? Why did some peoples cease to be primitives? What tremendous event, what revolution, allowed the figure of the Despot, of he who gives orders to those who obey, to emerge? *Where does political power come from?* Such is the mystery (perhaps a temporary one) of the origin.

While it still does not appear possible to determine the conditions in which the State emerged, it is possible to specify the conditions of its non-emergence; and the texts assembled in this volume attempt to delineate the space of the political in societies without a State. Faithless, lawless, and kingless: these terms used by the sixteenth-century West to describe the Indians can easily be extended to cover all primitive societies. They can serve as the distinguishing criteria: a society is primitive if it is without a king, as the legitimate source of the law, that is, the State machine. Conversely, every non-primitive society is a society with a State: no matter what socio-political regime is in effect. That is what permits one to consolidate all the great despotisms – kings, emperors of China or the Andes, pharaohs – into a single class, along with the more recent monarchies – "I am the State" – and the contemporary social systems, whether they possess a liberal capitalism as in Western Europe, or a State capitalism such as exists elsewhere ...

Hence there is no king in the tribe, but a chief who is not a chief of State. What does that imply? Simply that the chief has no authority at his disposal, no power of coercion, no means of giving an order. The chief is not a commander; the people of the tribe are under no obligation to obey. *The space of the chieftainship is not the locus of power*, and the "profile" of the primitive chief in no way foreshadows that of a future despot. There is nothing about the chieftainship that suggests the State apparatus derived from it.

How is it that the tribal chief does not prefigure the chief of State? Why is such an anticipation not possible in the world of Savages? That radical discontinuity – which makes a gradual transition from the primitive chieftainship to the State machine unthinkable – is logically based in the relation of exclusion that places political power outside the chieftainship. What we are dealing with is a chief without power, and an institution, the chieftainship, that is a stranger to its essence, which is authority. The functions of the chief, as they have been analyzed above, are convincing proof that the chieftainship does not involve functions of authority. Mainly responsible for resolving the conflicts that can surface between individuals, families, lineages, and so forth, the chief has to rely on nothing more than the prestige accorded him by the society to restore order and harmony. But prestige does not signify power, certainly, and the means the chief possesses for performing his task of peacemaker are limited to the use of speech: not even to arbitrate between the contending parties, because the chief is not a judge; but, armed only with his eloquence, to try to persuade the people that it is best to calm down, stop insulting one another, and emulate the ancestors who always lived together in harmony. The success of the endeavor is never guaranteed, for *the chief's word carries no force of law*. If the effort to persuade should fail, the conflict then risks having a violent outcome, and the chief's prestige may very well be a casualty, since he will have proved his inability to accomplish what was expected of him.

In the estimation of the tribe, what qualifies such a man to be chief? In the end, it is his "technical" competence alone: his oratorical talent, his expertise as a hunter, his ability to coordinate martial activities, both offensive and defensive. And in no circumstance does the tribe allow the chief to go beyond that technical limit; it never allows a technical superiority to change into a political authority. The chief is there to serve society; it is society as such – the real locus of power – that exercises its authority over the chief. That is why it is impossible for the chief to reverse that relationship for his own ends, to put society in his service, to exercise what is termed power over the tribe: primitive society would never tolerate having a chief transform himself into a despot.

In a sense, the tribe keeps the chief under a close watch; he is a kind of prisoner in a space which the tribe does not let him leave. But does he have any desire to get out of that space? Does it ever happen that a chief desires to be chief? That he wants to substitute the realization of his own desire for the service and the interest of the group? That the satisfaction of his personal interest takes precedence over his obedience to the collective project? By virtue of the close supervision to which the leader's practice, *like that of all the others*, is subjected by society – this supervision resulting from the nature of primitive societies, and not, of course, from a conscious and deliberate preoccupation with surveillance – instances of chiefs transgressing primitive law are rare: *you are worth no more than the others*. Rare, to be sure, but not unheard of: it occasionally happens that a chief tries to *play the chief*, and not out of Machiavellian motives, but rather because he has no choice; he cannot do otherwise. Let me explain. As a rule, a chief does not attempt (the thought does not even enter his mind) to subvert the normal relationship (i.e., in keeping with the norms) he maintains with respect to his group, a subversion that would make him the master of the tribe instead of its servant. The great cacique

Alaykin, the war chief of a tribe inhabiting the Argentinian Chaco, gave a very good definition of that normal relationship in his reply to a Spanish officer who was trying to convince him to drag his tribe into a war it did not want: "The Abipones, by a custom handed down by their ancestors, follow their own bidding and not that of their cacique. I am their leader, but I could not bring harm to any of my people without bringing harm to myself; if I were to use orders or force with my comrades, they would turn their backs on me at once. I prefer to be loved and not feared by them." And, let there be no doubt, most Indian chiefs would have spoken similar words.

There are exceptions, however, nearly always connected with warfare. We know, in fact, that the preparation and conduct of a military expedition are the only circumstances in which the chief has the opportunity to exercise a minimum of authority, deriving solely from his technical competence as a warrior. As soon as things have been concluded, and whatever the outcome of the fighting, the war chief again becomes a chief without power; in no case is the prestige that comes with victory converted into authority. Everything hinges on just that separation maintained by the society between power and prestige, between the fame of a victorious warrior and the command that he is forbidden to exercise. The fountain most suited to quenching a warrior's thirst for prestige is war. At the same time, a chief whose prestige is linked with warfare can preserve and bolster it only in warfare: it is a kind of compulsion, a kind of escape into the fray, that has him continually wanting to organize martial expeditions from which he hopes to obtain the (symbolic) benefits attaching to victory. As long as his desire for war corresponds to the general will of the tribe, particularly that of the young men, for whom war is also the principal means of acquiring prestige, as long as the will of the chief does not go beyond that of the tribe, the customary relations between the chief and the tribe remain unchanged. But the risk of an excessive desire on the part of the chief with respect to that of the tribe as a whole, the danger to him of going too far, of exceeding the strict limits allotted to his office, is ever present. Occasionally a chief accepts running that risk and attempts to put his personal interest ahead of the collective interest. Reversing the normal relationship that determines the leader as a means in the service of a socially defined end, he tries to make society into the means for achieving a purely private end: *the tribe in the service of the chief and no longer the chief in the service of the tribe*. If it "worked," then we would have found the birthplace of political power, as force and violence; we would have the first incarnation, the minimal form of the State. But it never works.

In the very fine account of the twenty years she spent among the Yanomami,[2] Elena Valero talks at length about her first husband, the war leader Fousiwe. His story illustrates quite well the fate of the primitive chief when, by the force of circumstances, he is led to transgress the law of primitive society; being the true locus of power, society refuses to let go of it, refuses to delegate it. So Fousiwe is acknowledged by his tribe as "chief," owing to the prestige he has obtained for himself as the organizer and leader of victorious raids against enemy groups. As a result, he plans and directs wars that his tribe undertakes willingly; he places his technical competence as a man of war, his courage, and his dynamism in the service of the group: he is the effective instrument of his society. But the unfortunate thing about a primitive warrior's life is that the prestige he acquires in warfare is soon lost if it is not constantly renewed by fresh successes. The tribe, for whom the chief is nothing more than the appropriate tool for implementing

2. Ettore Biocca and Helena Valero, *Yanoama*, Dennis Rhodes, trans., New York, Dutton, 1970.

its will, easily forgets the chief's past victories. For him, nothing is permanently acquired, and if he intends to remind people, whose memory is apt to fail, of his fame and prestige, it will not be enough merely to exalt his old exploits: he will have to create the occasion for new feats of arms. A warrior has no choice: he is obliged to desire war. It is here that the consensus by which he is recognized as chief draws its boundary line. If his desire for war coincides with society's desire for war, the society continues to follow him. But if the chief's desire for war attempts to fall back on a society motivated by the desire for peace – no society *always* wants to wage war – then the relationship between the chief and the tribe is reversed; the leader tries to use society for his individual aim, as a means to his personal end. Now, it should be kept in mind that a primitive chief is a chief without power: how could he impose the dictates of his desire on a society that refused to be drawn in? He is a prisoner of both his desire for prestige and his powerlessness to fulfill that desire. What may happen in such situations? The warrior will be left to go it alone, to engage in a dubious battle that will only lead him to his death. That was the fate of the South American warrior Fousiwe. He saw himself deserted by his tribe for having tried to thrust on his people a war they did not want. It only remained for him to wage that war on his own, and he died riddled with arrows. Death is the warrior's destiny, for, primitive society is such that *it does not permit the desire for prestige to be replaced by the will to power*. Or, in other words, in primitive society the chief, who embodies the possibility of a will to power, is condemned to death in advance. Separate political power is impossible in primitive society; there is no room, no vacuum for the State to fill.

Less tragic in its conclusion, but very similar in its development, is the story of another Indian leader, far more renowned than the obscure Amazonian warrior: I refer to the famous Apache chief Geronimo. A reading of his memoirs[3] proves very instructive, despite the rather whimsical fashion in which they were set down in writing. Geronimo was only a young warrior like the others when the Mexican soldiers attacked his tribe's camp and massacred the women and children, killing Geronimo's whole family. The various Apache tribes banded together to avenge the murders, and Geronimo was commissioned to conduct the battle. The result was complete success for the Apaches, who wiped out the Mexican garrison. As the main architect of the victory, Geronimo experienced an immense increase in his prestige as a warrior. And, from that moment, things changed; something occurred in Geronimo; something was going on. For, while the affair was more or less laid to rest by the other Apaches, who were content with a victory that fully satisfied their hunger for vengeance, Geronimo, on the other hand, did not see it that way. He wanted more revenge on the Mexicans; he did not believe that the bloody defeat of the soldiers was sufficient. But of course he could not go attacking Mexican villages all by himself, so he tried to persuade his people to set out again on the war path. In vain. Its collective goal – revenge – having been reached, the Apache society yearned for rest. Geronimo's goal, then, was a personal objective which he hoped to accomplish by drawing in the tribe. He attempted to turn the tribe into the instrument of his desire, whereas before, by virtue of his competence as a warrior, he was the tribe's instrument. Naturally, the Apaches chose not to follow Geronimo, just as the Yanomami refused to follow Fousiwe. At best, the Apache chief managed to convince (occasionally, at the cost of lies) a few young men with a craving for glory and spoils. For one of these expeditions, Geronimo's heroic and absurd army consisted of two men! The Apaches who, owing to the circumstances, accepted

3. *Geronimo: His Own Story*, S. M. Barrett, ed., New York, Ballantine, 1970.

Geronimo's leadership because of his fighting skill, would regularly turn their backs on him whenever he wanted to wage his personal war. Geronimo, the last of the great North American war chiefs, who spent thirty years of his life trying to "play the chief," and never succeeded....

The essential feature (that is, relating to the essence) of primitive society is its exercise of absolute and complete power over all the elements of which it is composed; the fact that it prevents any one of the sub-groups that constitute it from becoming autonomous; that it holds all the internal movements – conscious and unconscious – that maintain social life to the limits and direction prescribed by the society. One of the ways (violence, if necessary, is another) in which society manifests its will to preserve that primitive social order is by refusing to allow an individual, central, separate power to arise. Primitive society, then, is a society from which nothing escapes, which lets nothing get outside itself, for all the exits are blocked. It is a society, therefore, that ought to reproduce itself perpetually without anything affecting it throughout time.

There is, however, one area that seems to escape, at least in part, society's control; the demographic domain, a domain governed by cultural rules, but also by natural laws; a space where a life that is grounded in both the social and the biological unfolds, where there is a "machine" that operates according to its own mechanics, perhaps, which would place it beyond the social grasp.

There is no question of replacing an economic determinism with a demographic determinism, of fitting causes (demographic growth) to necessary effects (transformation of the social organization), and yet one cannot fail to remark, especially as regards America, the sociological consequence of population size, the ability the increase in densities has to unsettle (I do not say destroy) primitive society. In fact it is very probable that a basic condition for the existence of primitive societies is their relatively small demographic size. Things can function on the primitive model only if the people are few in number. Or, in other words, in order for a society to be primitive, it must be numerically small. And, in effect, what one observes in the Savage world is an extraordinary patchwork of "nations," tribes, and societies made up of local groups that take great care to preserve their autonomy within the larger group of which they are a part, although they may conclude temporary alliances with their nearby "fellow-countrymen," if the circumstances – especially those having to do with warfare – demand it. This atomization of the tribal universe is unquestionably an effective means of preventing the establishment of socio-political groupings that would incorporate the local groups and, beyond that, a means of preventing the emergence of the State, which is a unifier by nature.

Now, it is disturbing to find that the Tupi-Guarani, as they existed at the time of their discovery by Europe, represent a considerable departure from the usual primitive world, and on two essential points: *the demographic density ratio* of their tribes or local groups clearly exceeds that of the neighboring populations; moreover, *the size of the local groups* is out of all proportion to the socio-political units of the Tropical Forest. Of course, the Tupinamba villages, for instance, which numbered several thousand inhabitants, were not cities; but they did cease to belong to the "standard" demographic range of the neighboring societies. Against this background of demographic expansion and concentration of the population, there stands out – this too is an unusual phenomenon for primitive America, if not for imperial America – the manifest tendency of the chieftainships to acquire a power unknown elsewhere. The Tupi-Guarani chiefs were not despots, to be sure; but they were not altogether powerless chiefs either. This is not the place to undertake the long and complex task of analyzing the chieftainship among the Tupi-Guarani. Let me confine myself to pointing out, at one end of society, as it were, a demographic, growth, and, at the other end, the slow emergence of political power. It does not rest with ethnology (or at least not it alone) to answer the question of the causes of demographic expansion in a primitive society. But it does fall to that discipline to link the demographic and the political, to analyze the force exerted by the former on the latter, by means of the sociological.

Throughout this text, I have consistently argued that a separate power is not possible in a primitive society, for reasons deriving from their internal organization; that it is not possible for the State to arise from within primitive society. And here it seems that I have just contradicted myself by speaking of the Tupi-Guarani as an example of a primitive society in which something was beginning to surface that could have become the State. It is undeniable that a process was developing in those societies, in progress for quite a long time no doubt – a process that aimed at establishing a chieftainship whose political power was not inconsiderable. Things had even reached a point where the French and Portuguese chroniclers did not hesitate to bestow on the great chiefs of tribal federations the titles "provincial kings" or "kinglets." That process of profound transformation of the Tupi-Guarani society was brutally interrupted by the arrival of the Europeans. Does that mean that if the discovery of the New World had taken place a century later, for example, a State formation would have been imposed on the Indian tribes of the Brazilian coastal regions? It is always easy, and risky, to reconstruct a hypothetical history that no evidence can contradict. But in this instance, I think it is possible to answer firmly in the negative: it was not the arrival of the Westerners that put a stop to the eventual emergence of the State among the Tupi-Guarani, but rather an awakening of society itself to its own nature as primitive society, an awakening, an uprising, that was directed against the chieftainship in a sense, if not explicitly; for, in any case, it had destructive effects on the power of the chiefs. I have in mind that strange phenomenon that, beginning in the last decades of the fifteenth century, stirred up the Tupi-Guarani tribes, the fiery preaching of certain men who went from group to group inciting the Indians to forsake everything and launch out in search of the Land Without Evil, the earthly paradise.

In primitive society, the chieftainship and language are intrinsically linked; speech is the only power with which the chief is vested; more than that speech is an obligation for him. But there is another sort of speech, another discourse, uttered not by the chiefs, but by those men who, in the fifteenth and sixteenth centuries, carried thousands of Indians along behind them in mad migrations questing for the homeland of the gods: it is the discourse of the *karai*, a prophetic speech, a virulent speech, highly subversive in its appeal to the Indians to undertake what must be acknowledged as the destruction of society. The prophets' call to abandon the evil land (that is, society as it existed) in order to inherit the Land Without Evil, the society of divine happiness, implied the death of society's structure and system of norms. Now that society was increasingly coming under the authority of the chiefs, the weight of their nascent political power. It is reasonable, then, to suppose that if the prophets, risen up from the core of society, proclaimed the world in which men were living to be evil, this was because they surmised that the misfortune, the evil, lay in that slow death to which the emergence of power would sooner or later condemn Tupi-Guarani society, insofar as it was a primitive society, a society without a State. Troubled by the feeling that the ancient primitive world was trembling at its foundations, and haunted by the premonition of a socio-economic catastrophe, the prophets decided that the world had to be changed, that one must change worlds, abandon the world of men for that of the gods.

A prophetic speech that is still living, as the texts "Prophets in the Jungle" and "Of the One Without the Many" should show. The four or five thousand remaining Guarani Indians lead a wretched existence in the forests of Paraguay, but they are still in possession of the incomparable wealth afforded them by the *karai*. To be sure, the latter no longer serve as guides to whole tribes, like their sixteenth-century ancestors; the search for the Land Without Evil is no longer possible. But the lack of action seems to have encouraged a frenzy of thought, an ever deepening reflection on the unhappiness of the human condition. And that savage thought, born of the dazzling light of the Sun, tells us that the birthplace of Evil, the source of misfortune, is the One.

Perhaps a little more needs to be said about the Guarani sage's concept of the One. What does the term embrace? The favorite themes of contemporary Guarani thought are the same ones that disturbed, more than four centuries ago, those who were called *karai*, prophets. Why is the world evil? What can we do to escape the evil? These are questions that generations of those Indians have asked themselves over and over again: the *karai* of today cling pathetically to the discourse of the prophets of times past. The latter knew that the One was evil; that is what they preached, from village to village, and the people followed after them in search for the Good, the quest for the not-One. Hence we have, among the Tupi-Guarani at the time of the Discovery, on the one hand, a practice – the religious migration – which is inexplicable unless it is seen as the refusal of the course to which the chieftainship was committing the society, the refusal of separate political power, the refusal of the State; and, on the other hand, a prophetic discourse that identifies the One as the root of Evil, and asserts the possibility of breaking its hold. What makes it possible to conceive of the One? In one way or another, its presence, whether hated or desired, must be visible. And that is why I believe one can make out, beneath the metaphysical proposition that equates Evil with the One, another, more secret equation, of a political nature, which says that the One is the State. Tupi-Guarani prophetism is the heroic attempt of a primitive society to put an end to unhappiness by means of a radical refusal of the One, as the universal essence of the State. This "political" reading of a metaphysical intuition should prompt a somewhat sacrilegious question: could not every metaphysics of the One be subjected to a similar reading? What about the One as the Good, as the preferential object that dawning Western metaphysics assigned to man's desire? Let me go no further than this troublesome piece of evidence: the mind of the savage prophets and that of the ancient Greeks conceive of the same thing, Oneness; but the Guarani Indian says that the One is Evil, whereas Heraclitus says that it is the Good. *What conditions must obtain in order to conceive of the One as the Good?*

In conclusion, let us return to the exemplary world of the Tupi-Guarani. Here is a society that was encroached upon, threatened, by the irresistible rise of the chiefs; it responded by calling up from within itself and releasing forces capable, albeit at the price of collective near suicide, of thwarting the dynamic of the chieftainship, of cutting short the movement that might have caused it to transform the chiefs into law-giving kings. On one side, the chiefs, on the other, and standing against them, the prophets: these were the essential lines of Tupi-Guarani society at the end of the fifteenth century. And the prophetic "machine" worked perfectly well, since the *karai* were able to sweep astonishing masses of Indians along behind them, so spellbound (as one would say today) by the language of those men that they would accompany them to the point of death.

What is the significance of all that? Armed only with their Word, the prophets were able to bring about a "mobilization" of the Indians; they were able to accomplish that impossible thing in primitive society: to unify, in the religious migration, the multifarious variety of the tribes. They managed to carry out the whole "program" of the chiefs with a single stroke. Was this the ruse of history? A fatal flaw that, in spite of everything, dooms primitive society to dependency? There is no way of knowing. But, in any case, the insurrectional act of the prophets against the chiefs conferred on the former, through a strange reversal of things, infinitely more power than was held by the latter. So perhaps the idea of the spoken word being opposed to violence needs to be amended. While the primitive chief is under the obligation of *innocent* speech, primitive society can also, given quite specific conditions, lend its ear to another sort of speech, forgetting that it is uttered like a commandment: prophecy is that other speech. In the discourse of the prophets there may lie the seeds of the discourse of power, and beneath the exalted features of the mover of men, the one who tells them of their desire, the silent figure of the Despot may be hiding.

Prophetic speech, the power of that speech: might this be the place where power *tout court* originated, the beginning of the State in the Word? Prophets who were soul-winners before they were the masters of men? Perhaps. But even in the extreme experience of prophetism (extreme in that the Tupi-Guarani society had doubtless reached, whether for demographic reasons or others, the furthest limits that define a society as primitive), what the Savages exhibit is the continual effort to prevent chiefs from being chiefs, the refusal of unification, the endeavor to exorcise the One, the State. It is said that the history of peoples who have a history is the history of class struggle. It might be said, with at least as much truthfulness, that the history of peoples without history is the history of their struggle against the State.

This edition designed by Bruce Mau
Type composed by Canadian Composition
Printed by Provincial Graphics on
S.D. Warren's Olde Style acid-free paper
Bound Smyth-sewn by Martin Bookbinding